Beautiful
Animal Dolls

Beautiful Animal Dolls

Handcrafts
to
Treasure

Miriam Gourley

Sterling Publishing Co., Inc. New York
A Sterling/Chapelle Book

Chapelle Ltd.

Owner
Jo Packham

Editor
Karmen Quinney

Staff
Ann Bear, Areta Bingham,
Kass Burchett, Marilyn Goff,
Holly Hollingsworth,
Susan Jorgensen, Barbara Milburn,
Linda Orton, Leslie Ridenour,
Cindy Stoeckl, Gina Swapp,
Sara Toliver

Photographer
Kevin Dilley/Hazen Photography
Studio

Library of Congress Cataloging-in-Publication Data

Created by Akira Blount

10 9 8 7 6 5 4 3 2 1

Published by Sterling Publishing Company, Inc.,
387 Park Avenue South, New York, NY 10016
© 2001 by Miriam Gourley
Distributed in Canada by Sterling Publishing
⁒ Canadian Manda Group, One Atlantic Avenue, Suite 105
Toronto, Ontario, Canada M6K 3E7
Distributed in Great Britain and Europe by Cassell PLC
Wellington House, 125 Strand, London WC2R 0BB, England
Distributed in Australia by Capricorn Link (Australia) Pty Ltd.
P.O. Box 6651, Baulkham Hills, Business Centre, NSW 2153,
Australia
Printed In The United States
All Rights Reserved

Sterling ISBN-0-8069-6088-4

Page 1: Cirque du Giraffe created by Traci Benvegnu

If you have any questions or comments,
please contact: Chapelle Ltd., Inc.,
P. O. Box 9252 Ogden, UT 84409
(801) 621-2777 • FAX (801) 621-2788
e-mail: Chapelle@chapelleltd.com
website: www.chapelleltd.com

About the Author

Miriam Gourley's childhood was spent on a ranch in Southern Colorado, where she was extremely happy and content. Her parents had a positive influence on her, including their encouragement and interest in her artistic endeavors. Her father, in addition to running the ranch, was a carpenter; so there was never a shortage of tools, scraps of wood, nails, and imagination. Her mother was an artist, seamstress, excellent story-teller, and nurturer. Money was the only shortage they experienced, but lack of money helped Miriam and all of her siblings develop in a creative way.

For the past 18 years, Miriam has been a free-lance designer. She works with fabric, stuffing, batting, embroidery floss, ribbons, beads, paints, wood, paper, and just about anything else which might be transformed into something beautiful.

Miriam has designed projects for Cranston Print Work's website, V.I.P. Fabrics, Concord House Fabrics, Benartex Fabrics, and C.M. Offray & Son Ribbons. Her work has been featured several times in ads, and she has designed television projects for Fairfield Processing, Inc. In addition, she has taught doll-making, coproduced a television special for public television, lectured, coordinated cloth-doll exhibits, and has been featured in many magazines, including *Good Housekeeping*, *Woman's Day, Soft Dolls and Toys*, and others.

She has received a great deal of fulfillment in her career, and feels fortunate to be paid for something she loves to do.

Dedication

This book is dedicated to my parents, who created a wonderful place for me to experience childhood.

Contents

Created by Melinda Small Paterson

General Instructions

General Tools

The following materials and tools are needed to create the projects in this book. These materials and tools are not listed with the individual projects.

- Craft scissors
- Fabric scissors
- Pencil
- Sewing machine/coordinating thread
- Sewing needle/coordinating thread
- Straight pins
- Tape measure
- Tracing paper or photocopy machine

3. Stitch along pencil outline, leaving open as indicated on pattern.

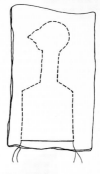

4. Cut around stitching, leaving ¼" seam allowance unless otherwise stated. Clip curves. Turn right side out and proceed, following individual project instructions.

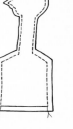

Patterns

Patterns for animal dolls and their clothing are full size.

All sewing for projects in this book is machine-stitched unless otherwise indicated.

Patterns Without Seam Allowance

1. Photocopy patterns at copy center or trace around patterns in book. Cut out patterns. Pin patterns onto appropriate doubled fabric with right sides together.

2. Using pencil, trace pattern onto fabric.

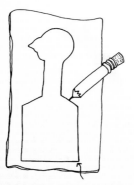

Patterns With Seam Allowance

1. Photocopy patterns at copy center or trace around patterns in book. Cut out patterns. Pin patterns onto appropriate fabric with right sides together.

2. Using pencil, trace pattern onto fabric, following individual project instructions.

3. Cut out pieces along pencil outline.

4. With right sides together, stitch around pieces, leaving ¼" seam allowance unless otherwise indicated. Clip curves. Turn right side out.

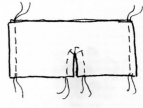

Stitching Techniques

Backstitch

1. Bring needle up between woven threads at A.

2. Go down at B, one opening to right. Come up at C. Go down at A.

Blind Stitch

1. Working from right to left with needle pointing left, roll hem edge under ¼". Take very small horizontal stitch next to hem.

2. Take next stitch in hem, ¼" to ½" to left of first stitch. Continue, alternating stitches. Make certain to keep stitches next to hem very small, and do not pull too tightly.

Buttonhole Stitch

1. Bring needle up at A; go down at B. Come up again at C, keeping thread under needle. Go down at D.

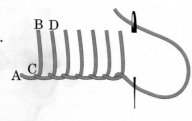

2. Repeat, making all stitches equal in size and shape.

Feather Stitch

1. Bring needle up at A; go down at B, and up at C. Alternate the stitches back and forth, working downwards in a vertical column.

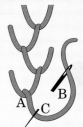

French Knot

1. Bring needle up at A. Smoothly wrap floss around needle once or twice. Hold floss securely to one side and go down at B.

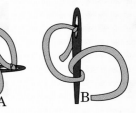

Ladder Stitch

1. Knot thread. Take needle down at first edge at A and come up to the left ¼" at B. At next joining edge, go down at C. Come up ¼" to the left at D. Go back to first edge and down at E.

2. Repeat, pulling tightly as necessary.

Satin Stitch

1. Bring needle up at A. Keeping thread smooth and flat, go down at B, forming straight stitch. Bring needle up at C; go down at D, forming another straight stitch next to the first.

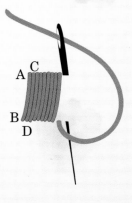

2. Repeat, filling design area.

Painting Techniques

Dry-brushing

Dry-brushing is used to apply color and shadows. For example, shadowed areas might include underneath eyebrows or lip areas.

1. Using stencil paintbrush, dip paintbrush into paint, then rub paintbrush back and forth on palette to distribute paint into paintbrush.

2. Rub paintbrush on paper towel or old rag to remove excess paint. When paint begins to have powder-like look, apply paint to project.

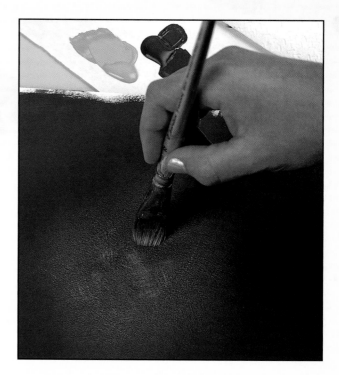

Floating

Floating is used to apply dimension by creating a highlight or shadow. *Tip: Wet the paintbrush in water that contains a few drops of color float.*

1. Using flat paintbrush, shake excess water from paintbrush, then dip one corner of paintbrush into paint. Rub back and forth on palette to distribute paint into paintbrush, then touch end of paintbrush to a paper towel if paint appears to be dripping.

2. Brush project area, starting along lower edge.

Spattering

Spattering is used to apply a light sprinkle of paint over an entire area. A toothbrush, fan paintbrush, or stencil paintbrush can be used. The fan paintbrush is cleaner, but in any case remember to put newspaper down to protect the work surface. *Tip: Practice before actually spattering a project.*

1. Using paintbrush, mix a little water into paint to slightly thin.

2. If using fan paintbrush, hit paintbrush hand near brush end. Otherwise, draw finger across bristles, causing paint to spatter onto painted project.

Created by Melinda Small Paterson

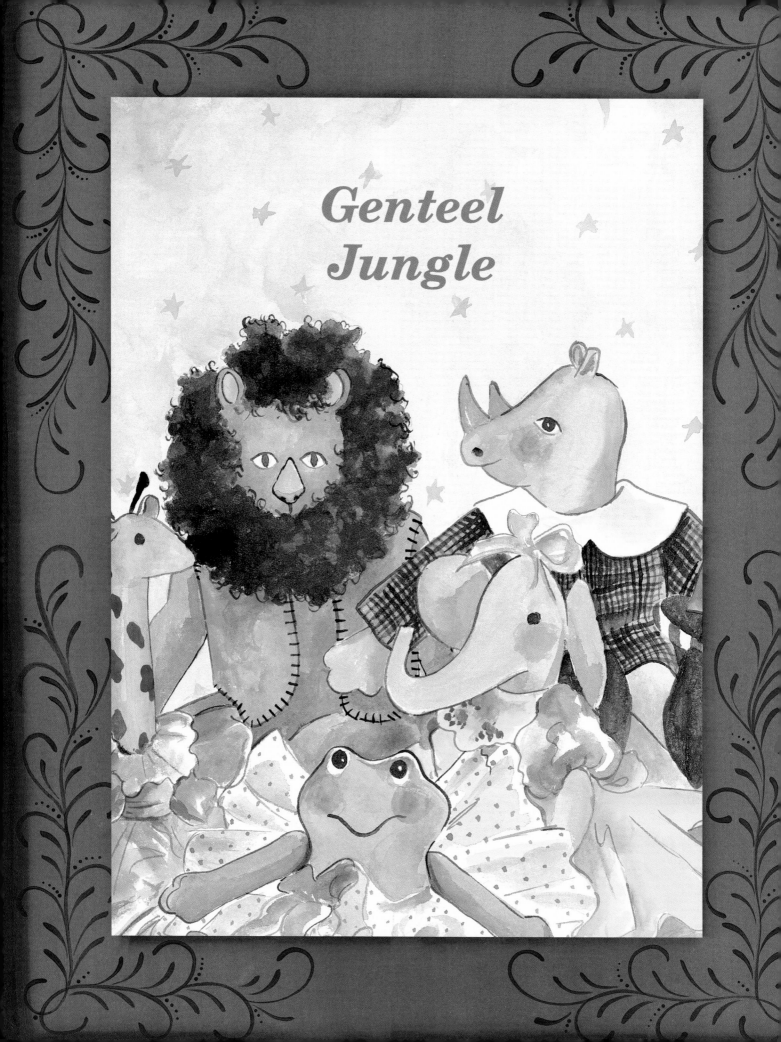

Genteel Jungle

Mephisto the Lion

Materials

- Acrylic paints: black; dk. brown; lt. cream; flesh; gold
- Bouclé yarn for mane and tail: brown
- Cotton flannel for body: taupe (⅓ yd.)
- Embellishment for vest as desired
- Embroidery floss to match felt for vest
- Felt scrap for vest
- Plastic pellets or birdseed (1½–2 cups)
- Polyester stuffing
- Sewing thread: black

Tools

- Hot-glue gun/glue sticks
- Needles: embroidery
- Paintbrushes: flat; liner; small stencil
- Tracing paper: white
- Transfer pen

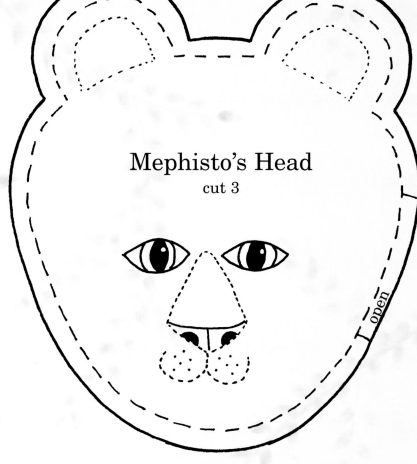

Mephisto's Head
cut 3

open

Instructions

Refer to Patterns on page 8 before beginning.

Head

1. Using transfer pen, trace Mephisto's Head pattern with nose and mouth outlines onto tracing paper. Using iron, transfer images to wrong side of single layer of flannel.

2. Place right side of traced head onto wrong side of second single layer of flannel.

3. Topstitch on nose and mouth lines with black thread. *Note: Stitching will be done on wrong side of flannel for head piece.* Cut out shape of head, cutting through both layers of flannel. See Diagram A.

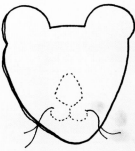

Diagram A

Continued on page 15.

Many jungle animals, like the lion, wear the newest and best clothing. It is very important to be well-groomed even if you do have the finest lion roar.

Continued from page 13.

4. Turn head over. Using tracing paper and transfer pen, transfer eyes and nose painting line to front side of face. Match stitched nose lines to face pattern.

5. Cut small slit in nose in flannel on wrong side of face and insert very small amounts of polyester stuffing to fill cavity. See Diagram B.

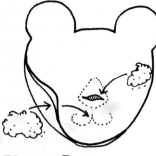

Diagram B

6. Insert small amounts of polyester stuffing between flannel layers into curved spaces below nose, forming upper lip.

7. With right sides of flannel together, place head on third single layer of flannel and stitch around head, leaving an opening for turning.

8. Clip corners by ears. Turn head right side out and insert small amount of polyester stuffing into each ear.

9. Topstitch ears. See Diagram C.

Diagram C

10. Finish stuffing head very firmly. Stitch opening closed.

11. Using flat paintbrush, paint inner ears and lower part of nose with flesh paint.

12. See Dry-brushing on page 10. Using stencil paintbrush, dry-brush upper lip area of face with flesh paint.

13. Using liner paintbrush, paint side areas of eyes with lt. cream paint. Paint iris area of eyes with gold paint. Paint pupil area

with black paint. Dot a small highlight in upper area of each pupil with lt. cream paint.

14. Using liner paintbrush, line eye with black paint. *Note: You may need to dilute paint a tiny bit with water to make an even line.* Fill in nose holes with black paint.

15. Using sharp pencil, dip sharp end into dk. brown paint and apply to upper lip in a freckle pattern.

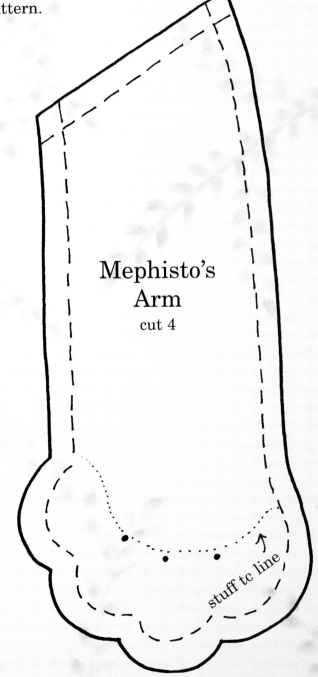

Mephisto's Arm

cut 4

stuff to line

15

16. Using pencil, trace Mephisto's Arm pattern and Mephisto's Leg pattern on pages 15–16 onto flannel. Cut out pieces.

17. With right sides together, pin pieces and stitch around sides and lower paw area, leaving top end open. Clip be-tween curved areas of paws. Turn right side out.

18. Stuff lower rounded areas of paws. *Note: There will be ½" or more of stuffing.* See Diagram D.

Diagram D

19. Using embroidery needle, knot thread at one end. Bring needle up between curves of paws at Point A, ½" from center point between curves. Wrap thread around area be-tween curves, bring needle up through first needle insertion point, then up through Point A. See Diagram E.

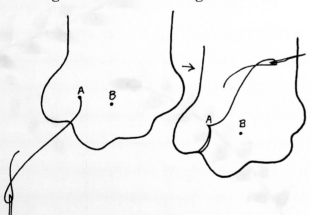

Diagram E

Mephisto's Leg
cut 4

stuff to line

20. Pull thread tightly and knot at Point A. Do not cut thread; insert needle close to knot, exiting at Point B. See Diagram F.

21. Reinsert needle, catch two or three threads to anchor it, and bring thread around end of paw as in Step 19. Repeat procedure until all three areas have been sculpted.

Diagram F

Mephisto's Body
cut 2

Robbie remembers his mother's birthday a week late.

insert legs

22. Pour ¼ cup of pellets into arm. *Note: The arm should be two-thirds full.* Fold raw edges inside upper edge of each arm and hand-stitch opening closed. Pour ½ cup of pellets into each leg. Machine-stitch across raw edges of each leg.

Body

23. Using pencil, trace Mephsito's Body pattern on page 17 onto flannel. Cut out body piece.

24. With right sides together, stitch around sides and neck of body. Clip angles by neck. Turn right side out. See Diagram I.

Diagram I

25. Pin legs to bottom edge of body so legs are curved outward, and toes are together. See Diagram J.

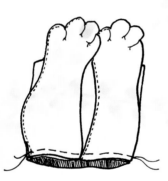

Diagram J

26. Stitch legs to body, then stuff body firmly. Fold lower edges of body inside and stitch opening closed. See Diagram K.

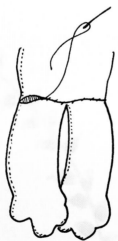

Diagram K

27. Stitch arms to shoulders, with largest curve of paws pointing outward. See Diagram L. Stitch head to neck.

Diagram L

28. Using flat paintbrush, paint pads on inside of all four paws with flesh paint.

Tail

29. Cut 1¾" x 5½" piece from flannel. Fold in half and stitch bottom and one side. Trim seam allowance. Turn right side out.

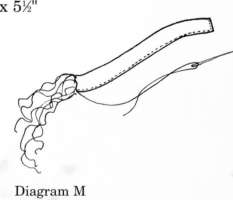

Diagram M

30. Cut several 6" strands of yarn and insert ends into open end of tail. Using embroidery needle, stitch yarn to tail with embroidery floss. See Diagram M. Stitch tail to back of lion, 2" above lower body seam.

Mane

31. Wrap yarn around four fingers six times. Slip yarn off fingers. Using short piece of yarn, tie around middle of bundle. Repeat for twelve bundles. See Diagram N. Hot-glue each bundle onto lion's head, starting at top, going behind ears, then around face and chin.

Diagram N

place on fold

Mephisto's Vest Back
cut 1

Mephisto's Vest Front
cut 2

Instructions for Clothing

1. Using pencil, trace Mephisto's Vest Front pattern and Mephisto's Vest Back pattern onto felt scrap. Cut out clothing pieces.

Vest

2. Place front and back vest pieces together, and stitch shoulder and side seams. Trim seam allowance.

3. See Buttonhole Stitch on page 9. Using embroidery needle, buttonhole-stitch around arm holes and outside edges of vest with embroidery floss.

4. Hot-glue embellishment onto front of vest. *Note: Pieces of leather, decorative buttons, or desired items can be used for vest embellishment.*

Abijah Montgomery III

Materials

- Acrylic paint extender
- Acrylic paints: black; med. brown; lt. cream; driftwood; dk. flesh; dk. gray; lt. gray
- Buttons: ⅝" (4); ⅞" (2)
- Cotton scraps: black for shoes; neutral for socks
- Crackle medium
- Gel stain: oak
- Linen scrap for collar: white
- Muslin for body: unbleached (⅓ yd.)
- Polyester stuffing
- Quilting thread: black
- Spray sealer: matte
- Velcro® fastener: small
- Woven cotton for clothing (⅓ yd.)

Tools

- Paintbrushes: flat; liner; stencil
- Paper towels
- Sanding pad: extrafine-grit
- Sculpting needle: 6"

Instructions

Refer to Patterns on page 8 before beginning.

1. Using pencil, trace patterns on pages 22–28 onto appropriate fabrics. The pencil lines will be the stitching lines for body only. Cut out all other pieces.

Body

2. Stitch around body and head, leaving bottom end open for turning. Trim seam allowance to ⅛" and clip curves. Turn body right side out.

Legs

3. With right sides together, place upper leg piece and sock piece together and stitch. Press seam allowance toward sock.

4. With right sides together, stitch shoe and sock together. Make certain foot is facing in the right direction. See Diagram A. *Note: Toes should point in opposite directions.* Press seam allowance toward shoe. Repeat Steps 3–4 for remaining leg pieces.

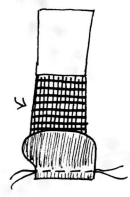

Diagram A

5. With right sides together, stitch two leg pieces together. Clip curves. Turn leg right side out. See Diagram B. Stuff leg firmly to within 2" of top opening. With front and back seams together, baste upper leg closed. See Diagram B. Repeat for remaining leg.

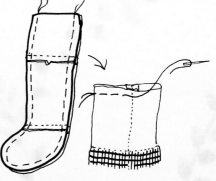

Diagram B

Continued on page 23.

ear

Abijah's Body

22

Continued from page 21.

6. With raw edges together, pin each leg to front of body, centering legs on edge of body opening with toes pointing toward body. Stitch legs to front edge of body.

7. Stuff body firmly. Fold back edge under. Hand-stitch opening closed.

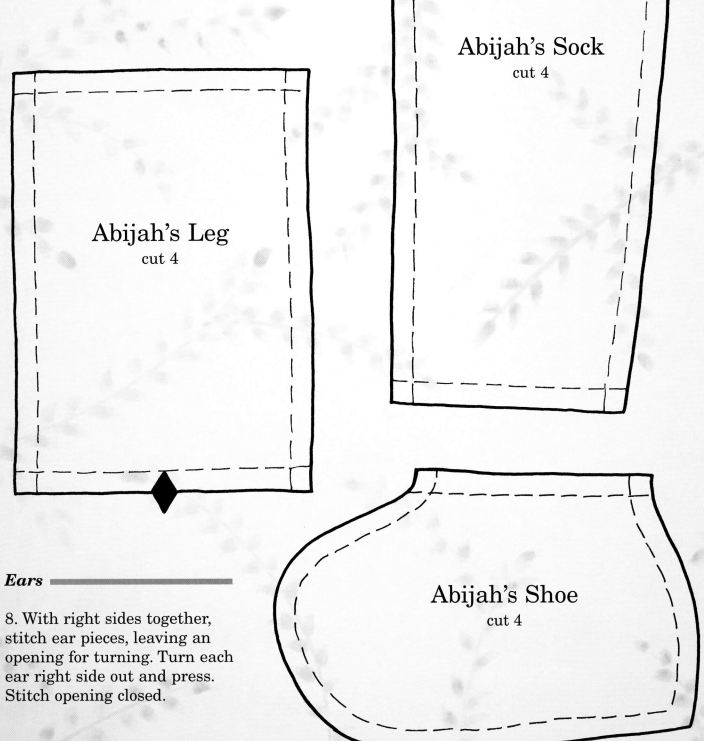

Abijah's Sock
cut 4

Abijah's Leg
cut 4

Abijah's Shoe
cut 4

Ears

8. With right sides together, stitch ear pieces, leaving an opening for turning. Turn each ear right side out and press. Stitch opening closed.

9. Fold ears in half and stitch together at base. See Diagram C. Hand-stitch to rhino's head as indicated on pattern.

Diagram C

Arms

10. With right sides together, stitch around each arm, leaving an opening at top. Clip curves. Trim seam allowance to ⅛". Turn arms right side out. Stuff firmly to within 2" of top with polyester filling.

11. See Ladder Stitch on page 9. Fold raw edges inside arm and baste together. Ladder-stitch arm to shoulder. See Diagram D.

Diagram D

Face

12. Using sculpting needle, create mouth and nose with quilting thread. Insert needle into cheek area and exit at corner of mouth. Pull thread until it disappears into cheek. At exit point, make two small catch stitches.

13. Bring thread around to front of mouth and insert needle into seam. See Diagram E. *Note: Dots on pattern are for thread placement.*

Diagram E

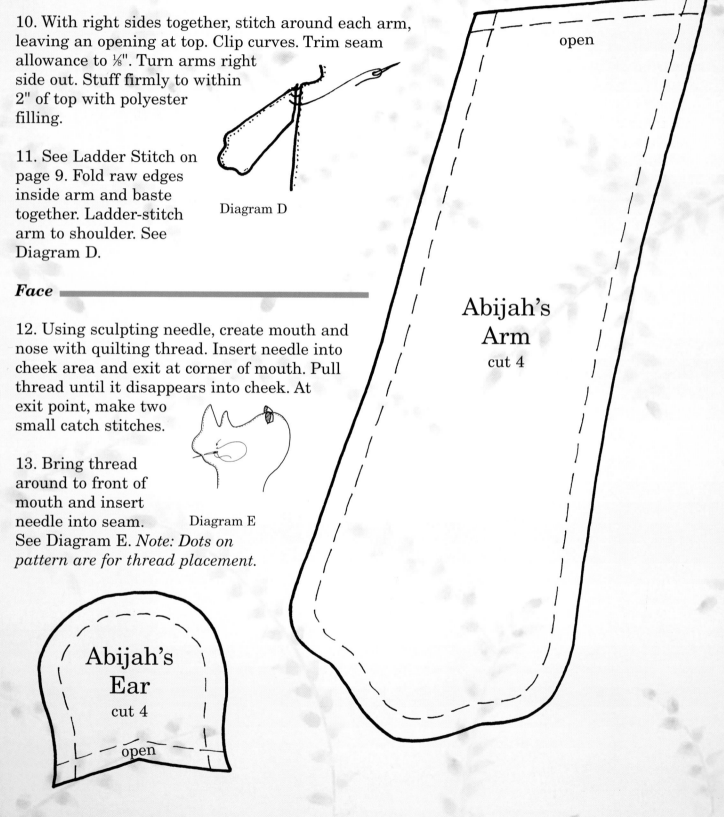

Abijah's
Arm
cut 4

open

Abijah's
Ear
cut 4

open

14. Continue thread around opposite side of head and insert needle into corner of mouth, through head, exiting at catch stitch. See Diagram F.

Diagram F

15. Repeat two times, pulling slightly to indent mouth. Knot and bury thread in rhino's head.

16. Insert needle through cheek and exit nose area to sculpt nose. Make two catch stitches and insert needle into nose, exiting from opposite side of head.

17. Reenter nose, just a fraction of an inch above exit point. Bring needle and thread back through head, exiting from catch stitch. Repeat this action two or three times, pulling slightly to indent nose area. Knot and bury thread in nose area.

Abijah's Bodice Front

cut 1

place on fold

Abijah's Bodice Back

cut 1

place on fold

18. Using flat paintbrush, base-coat rhino's head, neck, and hands with lt. gray paint. Let dry. Lightly sand surface to smooth. Apply second coat of lt. gray paint. Let dry. Using pencil, trace eye on each side of head.

19. See Dry-brushing on page 10. Using stencil paintbrush, dry-brush indented area of nose, and upper lip area, as well as shadows below and above eyes with dk. gray paint.

20. Using stencil paint-brush, dry-brush inside of ears and cheek area with dk. flesh paint.

25

21. Using liner paintbrush, paint upper eyelid with mixture of extender and dk. gray paint in 4:1 ratio. Let dry.

22. Using flat paintbrush, paint horns with a mixture of extender and driftwood paint in 1:1 ratio. Let dry.

23. Using liner paintbrush, paint iris with med. brown paint. Let dry. Paint pupils with black paint. Let dry. Paint whites of eyes with lt. cream paint. Let dry. Dot a highlight in pupil with lt. cream paint.

24. Using liner paintbrush, dot corner of each eye toward nose in with dk. flesh paint.

25. Mix water with dk. gray paint. Using liner paintbrush, paint a fine line to lower edge of eyelid.

26. When all paint is completely dry, brush on crackle medium, being careful not to overbrush. Let crackle medium air-dry for several hours.

27. Apply gel stain to painted surface. Using paper towels, immediately wipe off excess gel stain.

28. Spray painted surface with sealer.

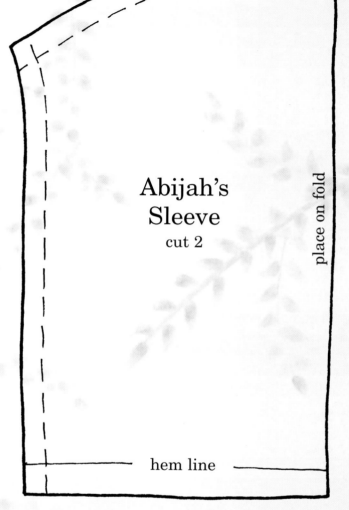

Abijah's Sleeve
cut 2

place on fold

hem line

Instructions for Clothing

Shirt

1. With right sides together, stitch bodice front and back pieces at shoulder seams. Press seams open.

2. Zigzag-stitch back edge of bodice and lower sleeve edges.

3. With right sides together, pin sleeve to arm opening and stitch at shoulder seam, easing in fabric. Trim seam allowance, and press seam allowance toward shoulder. Repeat for remaining sleeve.

4. With right sides together, stitch outer and back edges of collar. Clip center, and trim seam allowance to ⅛". Turn collar right side out. Press.

5. With right sides together, pin collar to shirt, matching neck openings, and fold back center edges of shirt ¼".

6. Stitch neck opening, clip corners, and trim seam allowance to ⅛". Zigzag-stitch raw edges together. Press seam allowance toward shirt. Turn back center edges of shirt right side out and press.

7. Fold collar upward and topstitch, just next to collar, stitching seam allowance to shirt.

8. Stitch Velcro fasteners to upper back corners of shirt, so edges overlap and collar ends are together.

9. With right sides together, stitch under-arm seams and clip corners. See Diagram A. Press seams open. Fold sleeve edges in ½" and stitch in place. Turn right side out and press.

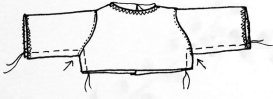

Diagram A

Trousers

10. Zigzag-stitch lower edges of trousers. With right sides together, stitch trousers together at front and back center seams. Clip curves and press seams open. See Diagram B.

Diagram B

11. With right sides together, matching center seams, stitch inseam and press seam open.

12. Fold hem up 1" and stitch in place. Press.

Ethel knits a wool sweater for her grand-daughter.

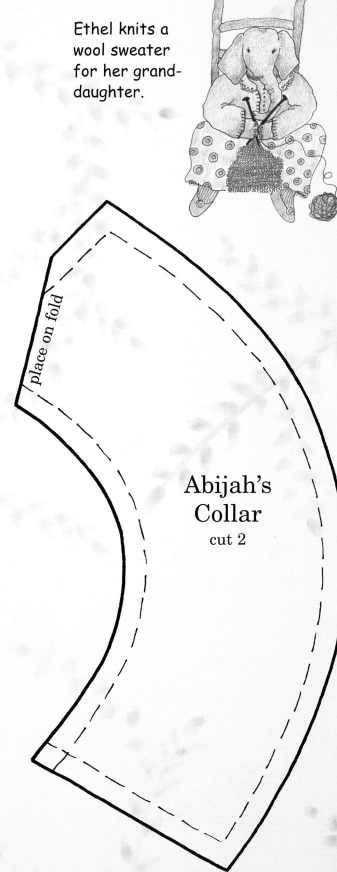

place on fold

Abijah's Collar

cut 2

13. With right sides together, matching center front of shirt to front seam of trousers, pin shirt and trousers together. See Diagram C. *Note: The shirt will overlap in the back.* Stitch shirt to trousers and press seam allowance toward trousers.

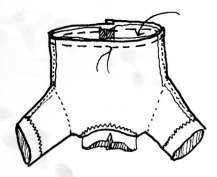

Diagram C

14. Stitch two buttons to each side seam of trousers, ½" above hem line. See Diagram D. Stitch remaining two buttons 1¼" from side seam of the shirt to top of trousers on seam line.

Diagram D

Abijah's
Trousers
cut 4

hem line

All dressed up in their finery and sitting carefully—so as to not wrinkle their party dresses, Miss Anne and Miss Ruth chat at an afternoon tea party.

Party Animals

Basic Body Instructions

Refer to Patterns on page 8 before beginning. *Note: Tape pattern pieces together as indicated before tracing onto fabric.*

1. Using pencil, trace patterns on pages 30–32 onto appropriate fabrics. Cut out all pieces.

Body

2. With right sides together, stitch body pieces together, leaving lower end open for turning. Clip curves, as necessary. Turn right side out.

Legs & Arms

3. With right sides together, stitch each leg, leaving top ends open for turning. Turn legs right side out. Stuff to within 2" of opening. Baste legs closed, matching front and back seams.

4. Pin legs to lower edge of body front, matching raw edges. *Note: The legs will almost touch each other at front center seam.* Stitch legs to body front.

5. Stuff body, beginning with trunk or neck, and inserting very small amounts of polyester stuffing in end of trunk or neck. When body is completely stuffed, stitch lower opening closed, enclosing raw edges inside body.

tape to top pattern piece

Miss Anne's Body
(bottom)
cut 2

ear

Miss Anne's Body

(top)
cut 2

tape to bottom pattern piece

7. Stuff arms firmly to within 2" of shoulder area. Stuff shoulder area very lightly. Stitch opening closed.

8. Thread doll-making needle with upholstery thread. Make stitch in arm where center of button should be. See Diagram A.

Diagram A

9. Insert needle into back side of button, then back through opposite hole and into arm. Continue through body and remaining arm. Make certain arms are evenly placed on body.

6. With right sides together, stitch arms together, leaving opening as indicated on pattern. Trim seam allowance and clip between thumb and finger area. Turn right side out.

10. Insert needle through back side of second button, then back through opposite hole, back through arm, body, and exit from hole of first button. See Diagram B.

11. Continue, going back and forth through body, arms, and buttons. Pull thread slightly to secure arms. Knot and trim excess threads.

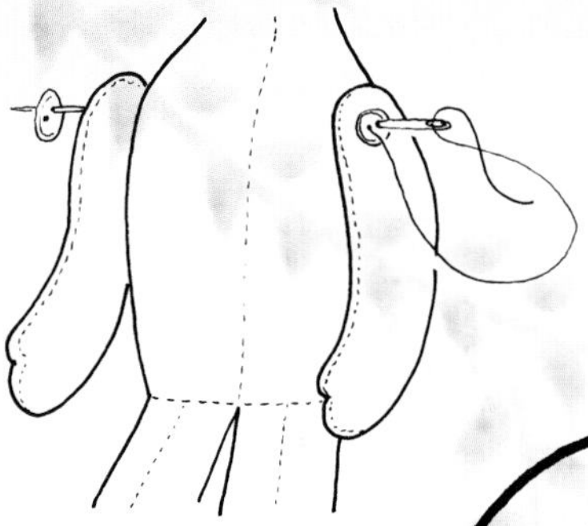

Diagram B

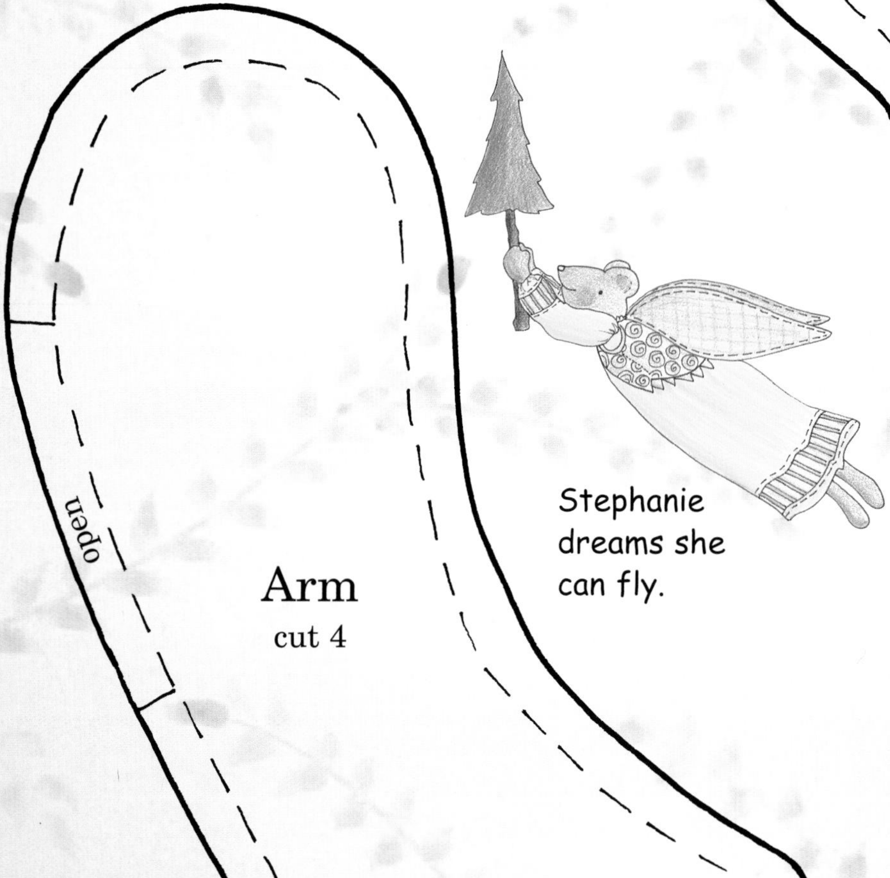

Stephanie dreams she can fly.

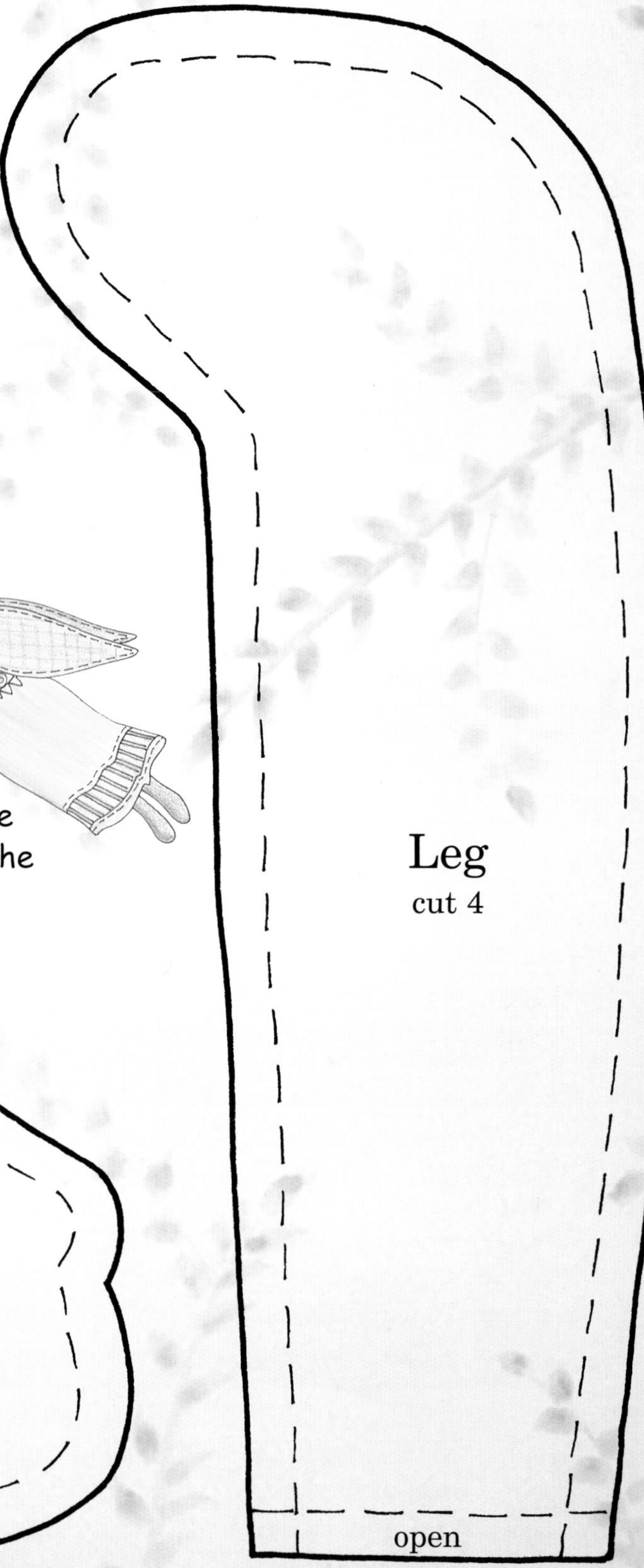

Arm
cut 4

open

Leg
cut 4

open

Face

12. Using doll-making needle, stitch one bead to each side of head, taking needle back and forth through head and pulling thread slightly to indent eye area. See Diagram C. When finished, make small knot next to bead and bury thread in head. Clip thread next to exit point.

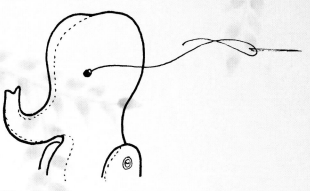

Diagram C

Miss Anne

- Acrylic paints: flesh; lt. gray
- Battenberg doily: heart-shaped, 4"
- Beads for eyes: black, 6 mm (2)
- Embroidery floss: mint green
- Flat buttons: ½" (2)
- Muslin for body: (⅓ yd.)
- Nylon tulle: apricot (⅓ yd.)
- Polyester stuffing
- Satin fabric for clothing: mint green (¼ yd.)
- Satin ribbon roses: small (5)
- Sheer ribbon: apricot for waistband, 5"-wide (1 yd.); for hair bow, 1½"-wide (¾ yd.)
- Spray sealer: matte
- Upholstery thread: heavy-weight

Tools

- Doll-making needle: long
- Hot-glue gun/glue sticks
- Paintbrushes: flat; small stencil

Miss Anne's
Ear
cut 4

open

Millie feels like she
is hung out to dry.

34

Instructions for Miss Anne

1. See Basic Body Instructions on pages 30–33. Create elephant.

2. Using pencil, trace Miss Anne's Ear pattern on page 34 onto muslin fabric. Cut out ear pieces.

Ears

3. With right sides together, stitch each ear together, leaving opening as indicated on pattern. Turn right side out. Fold raw edges of opening inside ears. Press ears and stitch opening closed.

4. See Ladder Stitch on page 9. Ladder-stitch ears to elephant's head, as indicated on pattern.

5. Using flat paintbrush, base-coat legs, arms, neck, head, and ears with gray paint. Let dry, then lightly sand painted surface.

6. Apply a second coat of gray paint. Let dry.

7. See Dry-brushing on page 10. Using stencil paintbrush, dry-brush inside of ears and cheeks of elephant with flesh paint. Let dry.

8. Spray painted surfaces with sealer.

Sleeve
cut 2

Instructions for Miss Anne's Clothing

1. Using pencil trace, patterns on pages 35–38 onto appropriate fabric. Cut out clothing pieces.

Sleeves

2. With right sides together, stitch shoulder seams, and press open.

3. With right sides together, gather-stitch top edge of sleeves. Pin gathered edge to sleeve opening. Stitch sleeve to bodice.

4. Zigzag-stitch neck opening, press hem under ¼" and stitch.

5. With right sides together, stitch side seams of bodice. Zigzag-stitch lower edges of sleeves.

Pants

6. Gather-stitch lower edge of pants to fit leg band. See Diagram A. With right sides together, stitch band to gathered edge of pants and press seam allowance toward band.

Diagram A

7. With right sides together, stitch front seam, and back seam. Clip curves and press seams open.

8. With right sides together, stitch inseam of pants and press seam open. See Diagram B. Press lower edge of band under ¼".

Diagram B

9. Fold band up to cover raw gathered edges. Stitch. Turn pants right side out.

Continued on page 38.

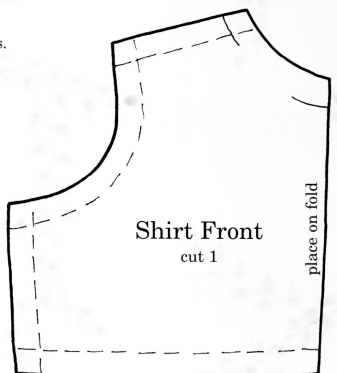

Shirt Front
cut 1

place on fold

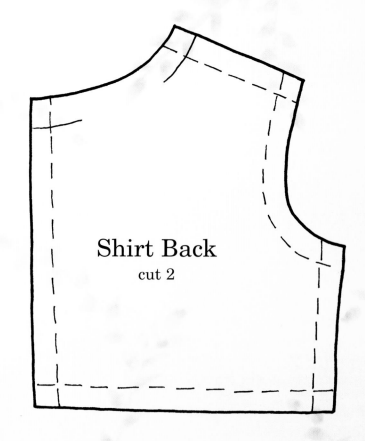

Shirt Back
cut 2

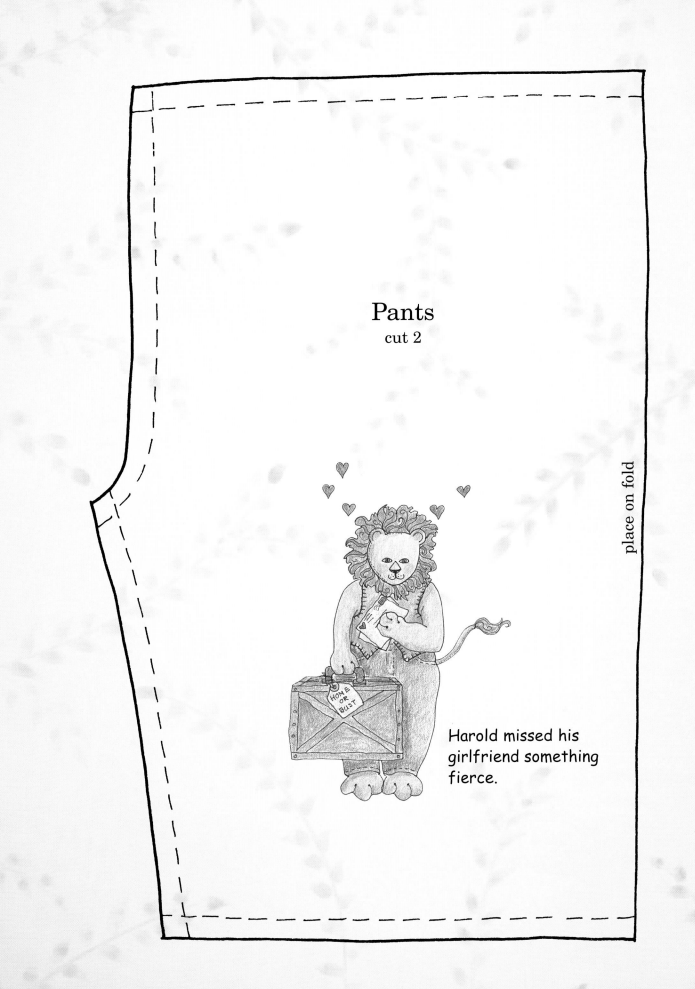

Pants
cut 2

place on fold

Harold missed his girlfriend something fierce.

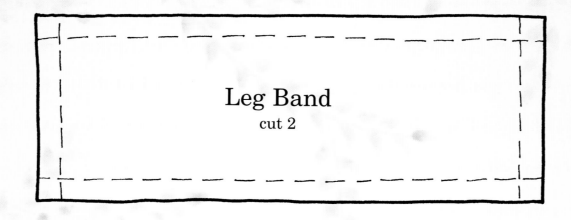

Leg Band
cut 2

Continued from page 36.

10. Using embroidery needle, gather-stitch upper edge of pants to fit lower edge of bodice with embroidery floss. With right sides

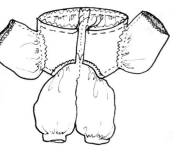

Diagram C

together, stitch pants to bodice and press seam allowance toward pants. See Diagram C. Press right back opening under ¼".

11. Gather-stitch ¼" above end of sleeves with embroidery floss.

12. Place pants on elephant, overlap right back edge over left. Stitch. Pull threads to gather ends of sleeves to fit elephant's arm. Push raw edges up into sleeve when gathering. Knot to secure.

Skirt

13. Cut 11" x 45" piece from tulle. Fold in half lengthwise. Using embroidery needle, gather-stitch folded edge with embroidery floss.

14. Gather tulle skirt around elephant's waist, with opening in back. Tie knot in thread to secure.

15. Tie long piece of ribbon around waist with large bow in back, covering gathered edge of tulle. Trim ties in an inverted-V shape. See Diagram D.

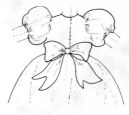

Diagram D

16. Fold heart-shaped doily 1¾" from edge of fold to top of heart. Cut pointed end off, leaving ¼" from folded edge. See Diagram E.

Diagram E

17. Stitch or glue folded edge at dress neckline. Hot-glue three ribbon roses onto collar; one at top center, and one on each of curved lower sections.

18. Hot-glue one ribbon rose at top, front center of each leg band.

19. Tie hair-bow ribbon around Miss Anne's ears, with bow on top of head. Trim ties in an inverted-V shape. *Note: The bow will be about 3½" wide.*

Miss Ruth

- Acrylic paints: golden brown; flesh; burnt umber
- Beads for eyes: black, 6 mm (2)
- Brocade ribbon: 1¼"-wide (¾ yd.)
- Chenille stem
- Embroidery flosses: gold; taupe
- Flat buttons: ½" (2)
- Muslin for body (⅓ yd.)
- Nylon tulle: taupe (⅓ yd.)
- Polyester stuffing
- Satin fabric for party suit: gold (¼ yd.)
- Semisheer wire-edged ribbon: antique gold, 1¼"-wide (15")
- Spray sealer: matte
- Upholstery thread: heavy-weight

Tools

- Doll-making needle: long
- Paintbrushes: flat; small stencil

Instructions for Miss Ruth

1. See Basic Body Instructions on pages 31–33.

Body

2. Using pencil, trace patterns on pages 39–40 onto appropriate fabrics. Create giraffe. Cut out all pieces.

horn

ear

Miss Ruth's Body
(top)
cut 2

tape to bottom pattern piece

3. Fold ears in half at base and stitch toge- ther. See Diagram A. See Ladder Stitch on page 9. Ladder-stitch ears to giraffe's head.

Diagram A

4. With right sides together, stitch horn pieces together. Carefully turn horns right side out.

5. Carefully stuff tiny bits of polyester stuffing into rounded ends of horns. *Note: Bamboo skewer or other small tool can be used to push the polyester stuffing in place.*

6. Fold 3" section of chenille stem in half, and insert into horn. See Diagram B. Push raw lower edges of fabric up into horn, then stitch horn opening closed.

Diagram B

tape to top pattern piece

Miss Ruth's Body
(bottom)
cut 2

Miss Ruth's Ear

cut 4

open

Miss Ruth's Horn

cut 4

7. Ladder-stitch horns to giraffe's head.

8. Using flat paintbrush, base-coat legs, arms, neck, head, and ears of giraffe with golden brown paint. Let dry, then lightly sand painted surface to smooth it.

9. Apply second coat with golden brown paint. Let dry.

10. See Dry-brushing on page 10. Using stencil paintbrush, dry-brush cheeks and inside of ears with flesh paint.

11. Paint horns and mottled pattern on neck, arms, and legs with burnt umber paint. *Note: The spots are rather loose diamond shapes.* Let dry.

12. Spray painted surfaces with sealer.

Instructions for Miss Ruth's Clothing

1. See Instructions for Miss Anne Steps 1–19 on pages 36–38.

Collar

2. Gather gold ribbon on wire along one edge. Pull both ends of wire at the same time, so ribbon does not slip off one end and make it difficult to gather. *Note: Be careful not to pull too hard, or the wire will break. If this happens, just remove the wire from one edge, and use a needle and thread to gather the ribbon.*

3. Gather ribbon to fit around neck, just above neckline. Twist wire in back of neck and hot-glue onto neck in two or three places, to keep from slipping.

*M*any years ago, it was reported that the Sun was going to be married. All the birds and the beasts were delighted at the prospect of a celestial wedding and quickly set about making preparations for an elaborate celebration.

Above all others, the Frogs were determined to honor the occasion with a festival of singing and dancing. Bedecked in all their finery, they were eagerly awaiting the glorious wedding day.

—Aesop Fable

Frogette

- Acrylic paint: dk. peach
- Embroidery flosses: black; white
- Felt scraps: black for pupil; dk. blue for iris; white for eye
- Fleece: mint green (⅛ yd.)
- Polyester stuffing
- Tulle: white with metallic gold dots, 6"-wide (4 yds.)
- Wired-edged ribbon: sheer with satin, 1½"- wide (1 yd.)

Tools

- Embroidery needle
- Paintbrush: small stencil

Instructions

Refer to Patterns on page 8 before beginning. *Note: Tape pattern pieces together as indicated before tracing pattern onto fabric.*

1. Using pencil, trace patterns on pages 44–46 onto appropriate fabrics. Cut out all pieces.

Face

2. Cut out two of each pattern below from appropriate felt scraps.

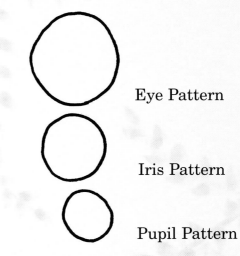

Eye Pattern

Iris Pattern

Pupil Pattern

3. Hand-stitch blue circle to white circle, creating eyes. *Note: The blue will be off-center, close to one side.* See Diagram A.

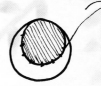

Diagram A

4. Hand-stitch black circle to one side of blue iris, creating pupils. See Diagram B.

Diagram B

5. See French Knot on page 9. Using embroidery needle, stitch French knot near edge of pupil with white embroidery floss, wrapping embroidery floss around needle three times. See Diagram C.

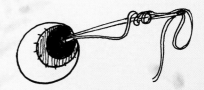

Diagram C

Continued on page 45.

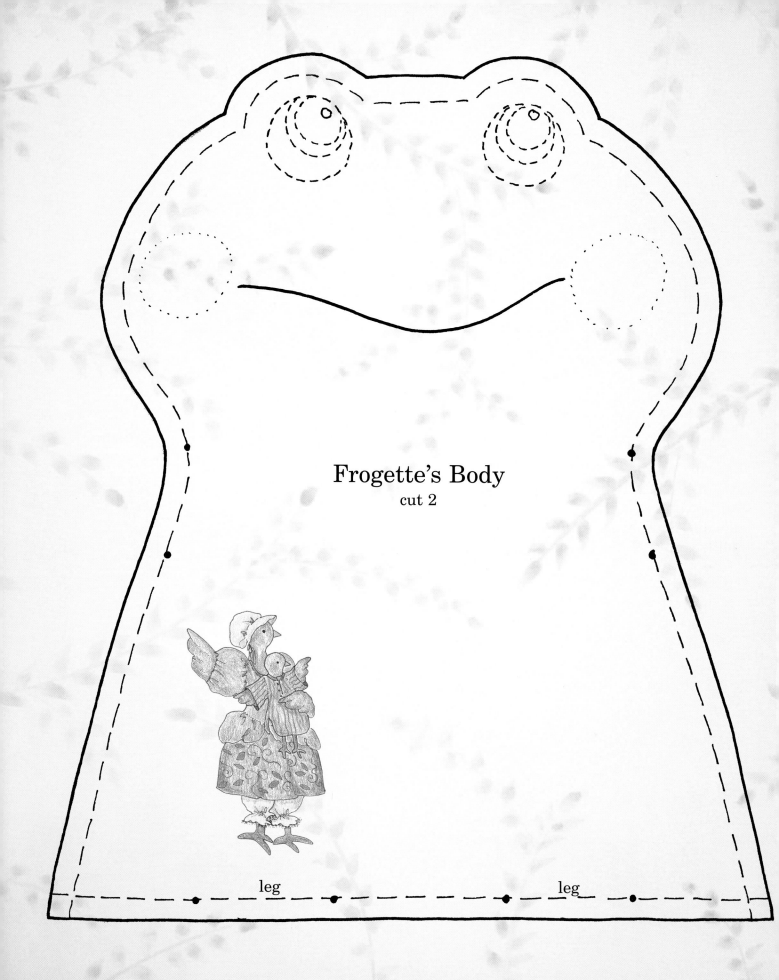

Frogette's Body
cut 2

leg   leg

Continued from page 43.

6. Stitch eyes to frog's face as indicated on pattern.

7. See Backstitch on page 9. Using embroidery needle, backstitch on face to create mouth with three strands of black embroidery floss.

8. See Dry-brushing on page 10. Using stencil paintbrush, dry-brush cheeks as indicated on pattern.

Arms, Legs & Body

9. With right sides together, stitch around arms, legs, and body. Turn right side out. Stuff arms and legs to within 2" of top.

10. Pin legs to bottom edge of body front as indicated on pattern. See Diagram D. Stitch legs in place.

Diagram D

11. Stuff body, then turn under back edge of opening and pin. Stitch opening closed.

12. Turn arm opening in ¼" and stitch opening closed.

13. See Ladder Stitch on page 9. Pin arm to body and ladder-stitch arm to seam, just below neck.

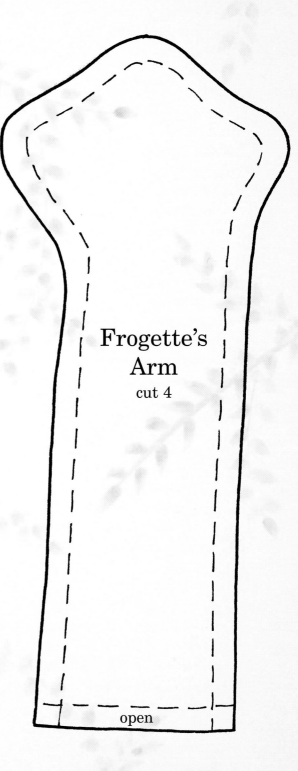

Frogette's
Arm
cut 4

open

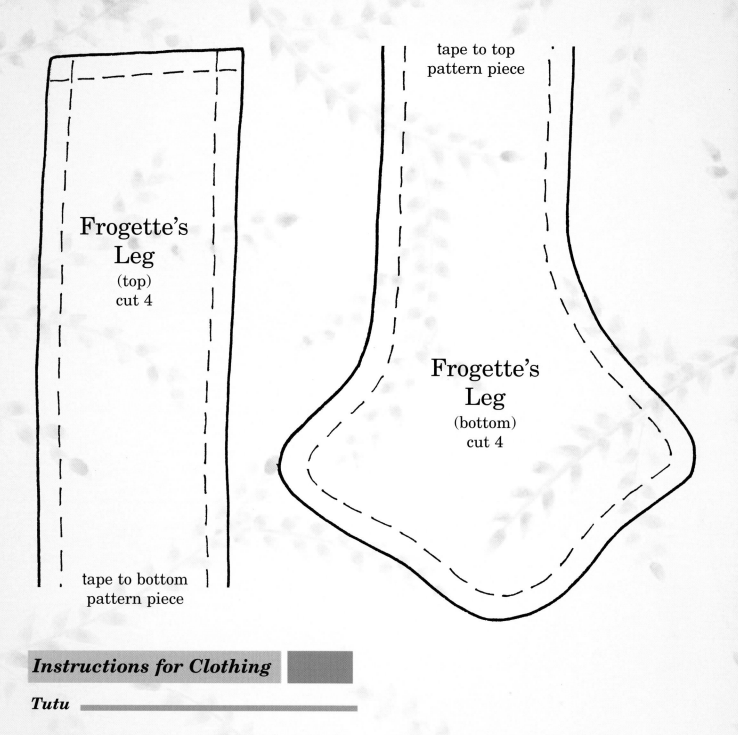

Frogette's
Leg
(top)
cut 4

tape to bottom
pattern piece

tape to top
pattern piece

Frogette's
Leg
(bottom)
cut 4

Instructions for Clothing

Tutu

14. Using embroidery needle, gather-stitch edge of tulle to fit around frog's waist, just under arms with white embroidery floss. See Diagram E. Pull gathers tightly and knot in back.

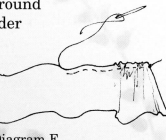

Diagram E

15. Tie ribbon around upper edge of tulle, covering gathered edge. Tack ribbon in place in several places.

16. Trim ends of ribbon to length of skirt. Trim ties in an inverted-V shape. See Diagram F.

Diagram F

Charming Countryside

Red Hen & Cocky Le Doodle

4. Topstitch wings as indicated on pattern pieces. Zigzag-stitch top edge closed. See Diagram A. Set wings aside.

Diagram A

Basic Instructions for Hen and Rooster

Refer to Patterns on page 8 before beginning. *Notes: Tape pattern pieces together as indicated before tracing pattern onto fabric. Muslin has no right or wrong side.*

1. Using pencil, trace patterns on pages 49–53 onto appropriate fabrics.

2. Stitch along lines, leaving openings as indicated on pattern pieces. Trim seam allowance to ⅛", clip curves, and turn all pieces right side out.

Wings

3. Lightly stuff wings, up to stitching line near open end of wings. *Note: There will need to be enough stuffing to make the wing thickness even, but not too much to prevent topstitching.*

Red Hen's Body
(top)

tape to bottom pattern piece

49

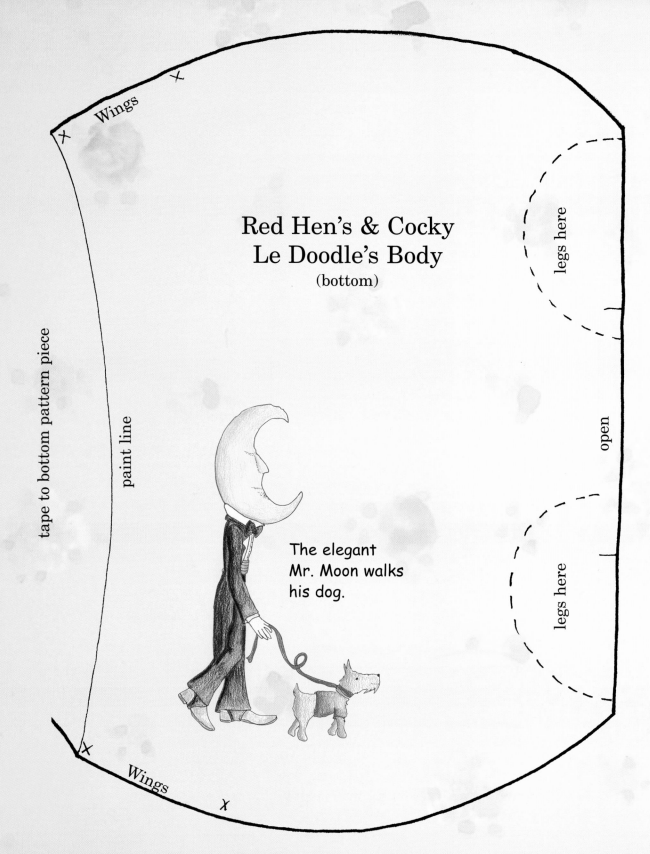

Red Hen's & Cocky Le Doodle's Body

(bottom)

Wings

X

X

tape to bottom pattern piece

paint line

legs here

open

legs here

The elegant
Mr. Moon walks
his dog.

Wings

X

Comb & Wattle

5. For hen, trace comb lines and wattle lines on body. Stuff small amount of stuffing into comb area and topstitch lower edge of comb. Repeat this step for wattle.

6. For rooster, trace comb lines and wattle lines on body. Stuff small amount of stuffing into comb area and topstitch lower edge of comb. DO NOT topstitch wattle. *Note: It will be stuffed later, to give rooster a larger looking neck.*

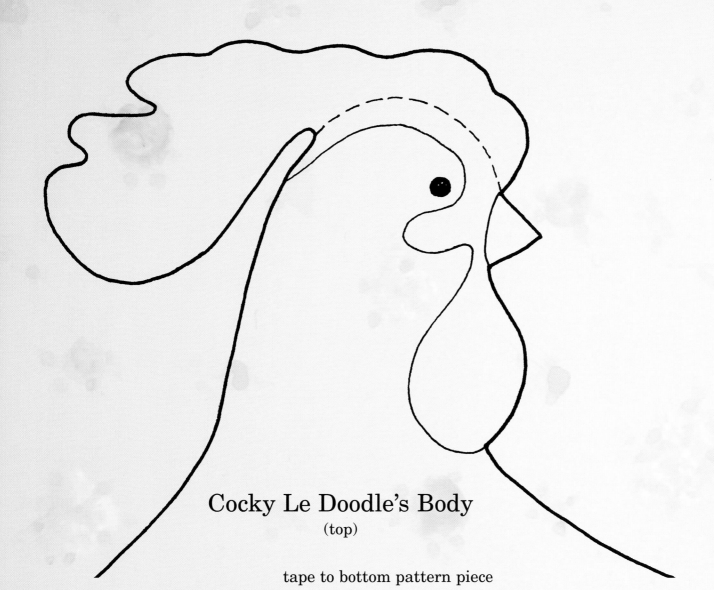

Cocky Le Doodle's Body
(top)

tape to bottom pattern piece

7. Finish stuffing remainder of body, then stitch lower edge closed.

Face

8. Stitch one bead to each side of head, taking needle back and forth through head and pulling thread slightly to indent eye area. Make a small knot next to bead and bury thread in head. Clip thread next to exit point.

Legs

9. Stuff legs to within ½" of knee line, then stitch across line. See Diagram B. Finish stuffing thigh area. Gather-stitch at top edge of drumstick. Pull gathers tightly and knot. See Diagram B.

10. Stitch legs to lower body as indicated on pattern. Make certain legs are placed so body will sit up.

11. See Ladder Stitch on page 9. Ladder-stitch wings to body at shoulders.

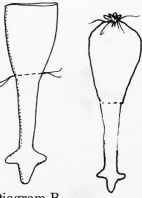

Diagram B

12. Insert stuffing inside upper tail feather area. Topstitch top section as well as lower area as indicated on pattern.

13. Carefully stuff lower areas of tail. Continue to stuff tail until firm.

14. Gather-stitch open end of tail and pull gathers tightly. See Diagram C. Set tail aside.

Diagram C

Red Hen

Materials

- Acrylic paints: black; med. gray; pigskin; moroccan red; taupe
- Antiquing gel: brown
- Battenberg doily for collar: 8"
- Beads: black, ³⁄₁₆" (2)
- Crackle medium
- Decorative button
- Embroidery floss to match bloomers
- Fabrics: for apron (¼ yd.); for bloomers (¼ yd.); for bow (scrap); for skirt (⅓ yd.); for sleeves (¼ yd.)
- Muslin for body (⅓ yd.)
- Polyester stuffing
- Spray sealer: matte

Tools

- Embroidery needle
- Hot-glue gun/glue sticks
- Paintbrushes: fan; flat; small stencil
- Paper towels

Wing

cut 2

paint line

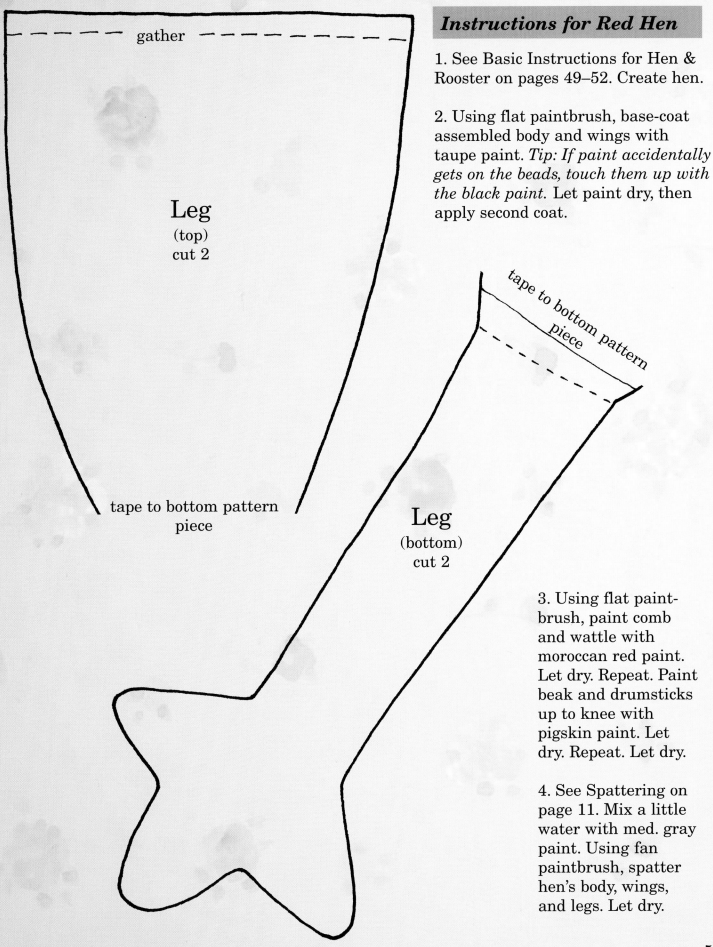

gather

Leg
(top)
cut 2

tape to bottom pattern
piece

tape to bottom pattern
piece

Leg
(bottom)
cut 2

1. See Basic Instructions for Hen & Rooster on pages 49–52. Create hen.

2. Using flat paintbrush, base-coat assembled body and wings with taupe paint. *Tip: If paint accidentally gets on the beads, touch them up with the black paint.* Let paint dry, then apply second coat.

3. Using flat paint-brush, paint comb and wattle with moroccan red paint. Let dry. Repeat. Paint beak and drumsticks up to knee with pigskin paint. Let dry. Repeat. Let dry.

4. See Spattering on page 11. Mix a little water with med. gray paint. Using fan paintbrush, spatter hen's body, wings, and legs. Let dry.

5. See Dry-brushing on page 10. Using stencil brush, dry-brush cheeks with moroccan red paint. Let dry.

6. Apply crackle medium on painted surfaces, following manufacturer's instructions. Let dry.

7. Using flat paintbrush, apply antiquing gel. Using paper towel, rub off excess gel.

8. Spray painted areas with sealer.

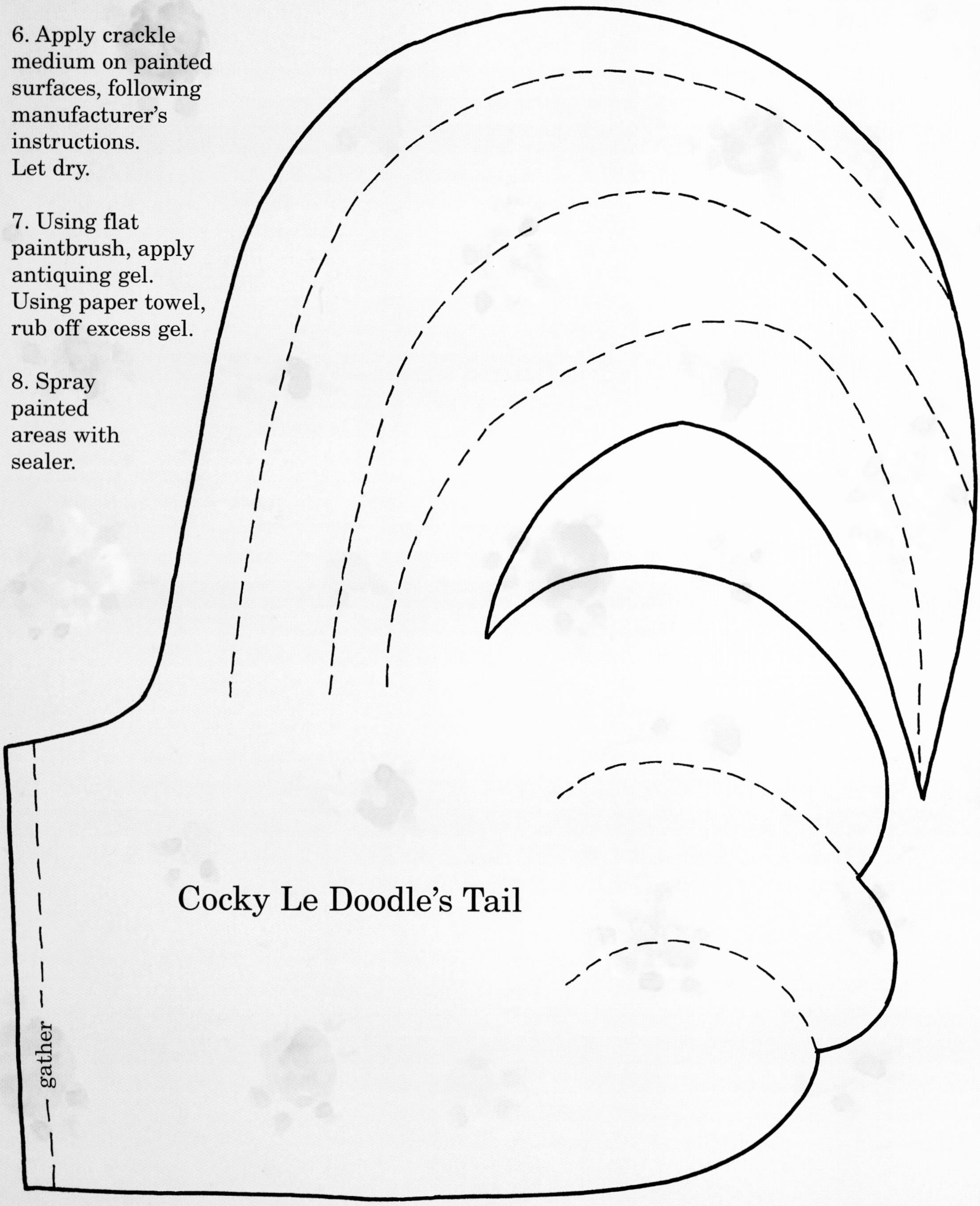

gather

Cocky Le Doodle's Tail

Instructions for Red Hen's Clothing

Bloomers

1. Tear two 8½" x 21" pieces from fabric. Place right sides together and pin. Find center and cut 4" slit lengthwise to make leg openings.

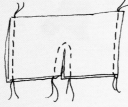

2. Stitch along 8½" sides and inseam. See Diagram A. Clip curves. Turn bloomers right side out and press.

Diagram A

3. Using embroidery needle, gather-stitch around waist with embroidery floss. Knot. Gather-stitch bottom edge of leg openings, 1" from raw edge, to fit around knee seam of chicken. Pull gathers tightly and knot.

Sleeves & Skirt

4. Tear two 8¼" x 22" pieces from fabric for sleeves. With right sides together, stitch each sleeve along 8¼" edge. Press seam open, and gather-stitch along both top and bottom edges. Place sleeves on hen, pull gathers tightly, and tack in place at shoulders. See Diagram B.

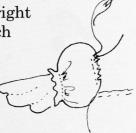

Diagram B

5. Tear 9¼" x 45" piece from fabric for skirt. With right sides together, stitch back seam along 9¼" edge. See Diagram C. Press seam open and place on table so the back seam is exactly in center of skirt. Slit each side 2½" lengthwise from top edge.

Diagram C

6. Gather-stitch front and back separately. Tie floss in a knot over shoulders. *Note: The slits will accommodate hen's wings and sleeves.*

Apron

7. Tear 7½" x 45" piece from fabric. Repeat Steps 5–6 to finish apron.

8. Tuck raw edges of apron sleeves inside and tack sleeves to apron slits.

9. Cut a neck opening in doily to fit over hen's head and rest on neck gathers of apron. Zigzag-stitch around opening and place collar on hen. Hot-glue to keep from slipping.

10. Tear 2" strip from fabric. Press and tie into a bow. Hot-glue onto collar of hen. Hot-glue button to center of bow.

55

Cocky Le Doodle

Materials

- Acrylic paints: black; med. gray; pigskin; moroccan red; taupe
- Antiquing gel: brown
- Beads: black, ³⁄₁₆" (2)
- Buttons: ½" (4)
- Crackle medium
- Embroidery floss: black
- Fabrics: for overalls (¼ yd.); for peasant shirt (⅛ yd.)
- Muslin for body (⅛ yd.)
- Polyester stuffing
- Quilting thread: gray
- Spray sealer: matte

Tools

- Hot-glue gun/glue sticks
- Paintbrushes: fan; flat; small round stencil

Instructions for Cocky Le Doodle

1. See Basic Instructions for Hen & Rooster on pages 49–52 and 54. Create rooster. Stitch tail onto back of body so tail rests even with base of body.

2. Using flat paintbrush, base-coat head and neck of body, tail, and wings with black paint. Let dry, then apply second coat.

3. See Dry-brushing on page 10. *Note: Do not rub much of the paint out before rubbing the brush onto rooster.* Using stencil paintbrush, dry-brush body, tail, and wings with taupe paint. Avoid getting paint into crevices made by topstitching. *Note: The black which peeks through in these areas will achieve the appearance of darker feathers underneath the surface.*

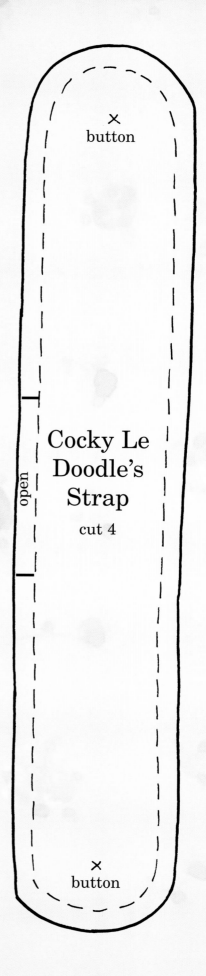

button

Cocky Le
Doodle's
Strap

cut 4

open

button

4. Follow Instructions for Red Hen Steps 2–7 on pages 53–54 to finish painting rooster.

5. Using pencil, trace patterns on pages 56–57 onto appropriate fabrics. Cut out clothing pieces.

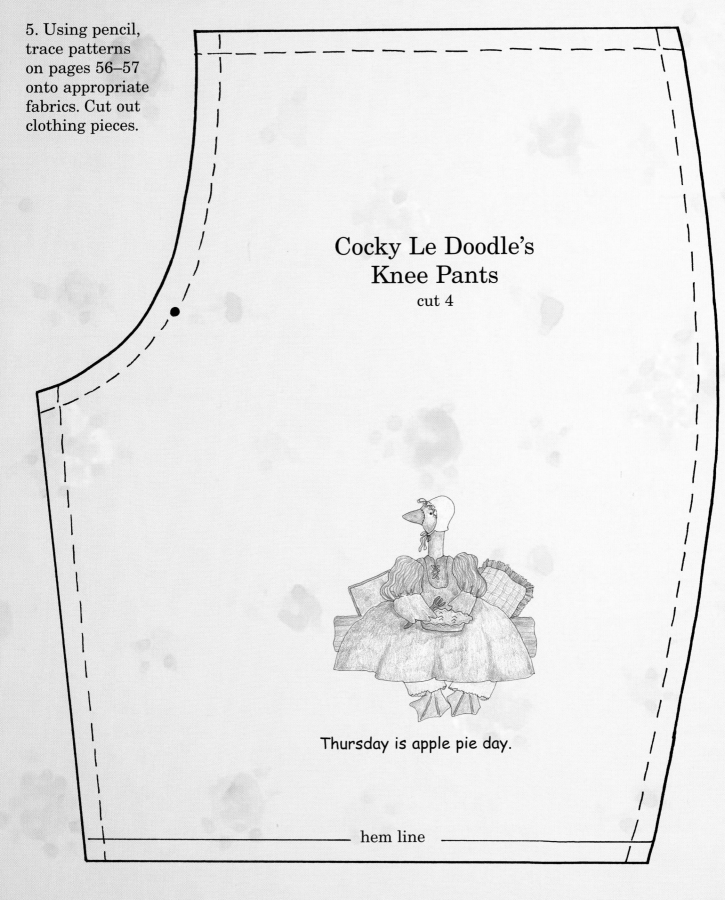

Cocky Le Doodle's Knee Pants
cut 4

Thursday is apple pie day.

hem line

Instructions for Cocky Le Doodle's Clothing

Knee Pants & Shirt

1. With right sides together, stitch front curved seam of knee pants. Repeat for back seam. Clip curves and press seams open.

2. Cut 5" x 18½" piece from fabric for shirt front. Cut two 5" x 9¼" pieces from fabric for shirt back. Cut two 4½" x 20" pieces from fabric for sleeves.

3. Gather-stitch lower edge of shirt front to fit top edge of knee pants. With right sides together, stitch shirt front to pants. Press seam toward pants. See Diagram A.

Diagram A

Sadie learns how to polish apples.

4. Gather-stitch lower edge of each shirt back to fit pants back. With right sides together, stitch shirt backs to back edges of knee pants.

5. Press seams toward knee pants.

6. With right sides together, stitch top edge of shirt 1½" inward from edge. *Note: This will form shoulder seams, leaving a neck opening.*

7. Press under ¼" hem around neck opening, and press shoulder seams open.

8. Gather-stitch one long edge of each sleeve. With right sides together, pin gathers to fit side edges of shirt, ending at top edge of knee pants. Stitch sleeve to shirt. Press seam allowance toward sleeve.

9. With right sides together, stitch side and underarm seams of shirt and knee pants. Stitch inseam. See Diagram B. Clip curves and under arms. Turn clothing right side out and press. Press hem under ¼" on lower edges of knee pants.

Diagram B

10. Using embroidery needle, gather-stitch around sleeve openings, beginning and ending at top of sleeve with embroidery floss. Gather-stitch around leg openings.

11. Knot end of floss. Gather-stitch from back neck opening to center of shirt front. Cut thread at center front, leaving 5"–6" tail. Repeat for opposite side of neck opening.

12. Place clothing on rooster and pull gathers tight around knee. Knot securely and trim embroidery floss close to knot.

13. Stitch back opening closed with quilting thread, fitting around tail. Pull gathered neck edge tightly and tie a bow with em-broidery floss. Trim excess embroidery floss and knot ends.

14. Pull gathers tightly around sleeves, pushing sleeves midway up wing. Tie a bow with embroidery floss. Trim excess em-broidery floss and knot each end.

15. With right sides together, stitch around straps, leaving opening as indicated on pattern. Trim seam allowance, turn strap right side out, and press. Stitch opening closed.

16. Stitch one button to each end of strap. Hot-glue strap to front of rooster's pants, overlapping seam. See Diagram C. Hot-glue remaining end to back, and repeat for remaining strap.

Diagram C

Fairy Goose-Mother

Materials

- Acrylic paints: lt. gold; raspberry
- Battenberg doily for collar: 6"-square
- Beads for eyes: black, ¼" (2)
- Buttons: white, ⅞" (2)
- Coordinating thread
- Cotton fabrics: off-white for body, star, wings (½ yd.); print for bloomers (⅓ yd.); print for petticoat (⅛ yd.); print for skirt and sleeves (⅔ yd.); pumpkin-colored print for legs (½ yd.)
- Craft glue: white
- Embroidery floss: pumpkin
- Felt scrap for beak: pumpkin
- Polyester stuffing
- Quilting thread: off-white
- Satin ribbon for bow at neck: ⅞"-wide (⅓ yd.)
- Sheer ribbon for bonnet/ bloomers: 1½"-wide (1⅓ yds.)

Fairy
Goose-Mother's
Body
(top)

tape on bottom pattern
piece

- Straw bonnet: 3½"-dia.
- Thread scraps: metallic
- Wooden dowel: ⅛"-dia. (6")

Tools

- Needles: embroidery; sculpting, 6"
- Paintbrushes: flat; small stencil

tape to top pattern piece

x
button

Fairy
Goose-Mother's Body
(bottom)

x   leg   x   x   leg   x

Instructions

Refer to Patterns on page 8 before beginning.
*Note: Tape pattern pieces together as indicated
before tracing pattern onto fabric.*

1. Using pencil, trace patterns on pages 61–66 onto
appropriate fabrics. The pencil outline will be the
stitching line for body only. Cut out all other pieces.

Body

2. Stitch around body, leaving bottom end open for
turning. Trim seam allowance to ⅛" and clip curves.
Turn body right side out.

Legs

3. Stitch around sides and bottom
of each leg. Clip curves. Turn
legs right side out. Press
each leg.

4. Topstitch top of each
foot. See Diagram A.
Stuff leg firmly to within
1" of knee line. Topstitch
across knee line, then
continue stuffing leg to
within 1" of open end.

Diagram A

Fairy
Goose-
Mother's
Leg

(top)
cut 4

tape to
bottom
piece

tape to top
pattern piece

Fairy
Goose-
Mother's
Leg

(bottom)
cut 4

5. Pin legs to bottom edge of body front. Stitch legs in place.

6. Begin stuffing head very firmly, working down into body area. *Note: As you stuff the body, the head may become a bit wobbly.* Push polyester stuffing firmly toward shoulders and neck.

7. Using sculpting needle, stitch one button to each side of body, passing needle and thread through body and pulling threads tightly. See Diagram B. Go back and forth through body several times.

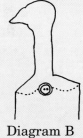

Diagram B

8. Continue stuffing body until firm. Fold raw edge on back of body inward and stitch opening closed.

Wings

9. Stitch around outside of wing, leaving opening at top. Clip curves. Turn wing right side out and press. Mark topstitch lines.

10. Insert small amount of polyester stuffing into bottom tips of wing. Top-stitch. Continue stuffing wing to within 1" of area where wing narrows. See Diagram C. Topstitch across wing.

Diagram C

11. Fold raw edges of wing inside. See Ladder Stitch on page 9. Ladder-stitch wing to shoulder, with longest tip of wings even with shoulders. See Diagram D.

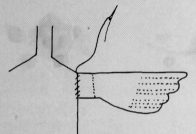

Diagram D

Face

12. Stitch felt beak together. Trim to a very narrow seam allowance. Turn beak right side out. Place beak on head. Adjust beak until it fits correctly.

Fairy Goose-Mother's Beak

cut 2

13. See Buttonhole Stitch on page 9. Using embroidery needle, buttonhole-stitch beak to goose's head with embroidery floss.

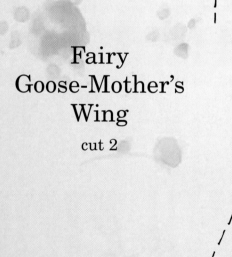

Fairy Goose-Mother's Wing

cut 2

open

14. Using sculpting needle, stitch one bead to each side of head, taking needle back and forth through head and pulling thread slightly to indent eye area. When finished, make a small knot next to bead and bury thread in head. Clip thread at exit point.

15. See Dry-brushing on page 10. Using stencil paintbrush, dry-brush cheeks with raspberry paint.

Instructions for Clothing

Bloomers

1. Cut two 12" x 14" rectangles from fabric. Cut 7" slit up the middle, then stitch sides and inseam. See Diagram A. Clip curves. Turn bloomers right side out. Press.

Diagram A

2. Using embroidery needle, gather-stitch around waist with embroidery floss. Place on goose's waist. Pull gathers tightly and tack, attaching bloomers to goose's body.

3. Gather-stitch lower edges of leg openings to fit around goose's lower legs.

Petticoat

4. Tear 10" x 45" piece from fabric. With right sides together, stitch 10" ends together. Press seam open.

5. Turn right side out. Using embroidery needle, gather-stitch around waist with embroidery floss. Pull gathers tightly and tack, attaching body above bloomers. See Diagram B. *Note: The lower edge doesn't have to be hemmed, but can be stitched with a decorative running stitch around the lower edge as desired.*

Diagram B

Sleeves

6. Cut two 8" x 20" rectangles from fabric. With right sides together, stitch 8" edges together. Press seam open. Turn right side out.

7. Gather-stitch both ends and pull gathers to fit around shoulder area. Tack gathers to shoulder. Pull gathers to fit around middle of wing. Pull gathers tightly. See Diagram C. Tack to wing.

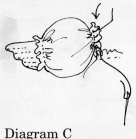
Diagram C

Skirt

8. Cut 10½" x 45" piece from fabric. With right sides together, stitch 10½" edges together. Press seam open. Turn right side out. With seam in center back, make 4½" slit at each side for arm openings. See Diagram D.

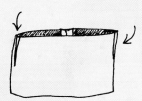
Diagram D

9. Gather-stitch neck edge, continuing gathering over slits. Place on goose. Pull gathers tightly around neck. Knot. Tack sleeve openings over raw edges of sleeves to hide them.

10. Tie sheer ribbon around raw edges of bloomers into a 2½"-wide bow. Trim ties in an inverted-V shape.

11. Place straw bonnet on goose's head and center sheer ribbon over top of bonnet. Tack bonnet and ribbon to goose's head with quilting thread.

Collar

12. Using Neck Template, cut an oval shape in the doily. *Note: The slit is approximately 2" long. See Diagram E.* Place on goose's neck, just over skirt gathers, then overlap collar edges in back and tack them to goose's body.

Diagram E

13. Tie bow from satin ribbon. *Note: The bow will be approximately 3" wide with 2½" ties.* Trim ends of ties at 45° angle. Tack or glue to front of collar at neckline.

Wand

14. Stitch star together, leaving small opening for turning. Clip angles and trim pointed ends of star. Turn star right side out.

15. Stuff star. Stitch opening closed.

16. Using flat paintbrush, paint dowel with raspberry paint. Let dry.

17. Using flat paintbrush, paint star with lt. gold paint. Let dry.

18. Clip very small hole at one intersecting point on star. Apply craft glue to end of dowel. Push dowel inside.

19. Cut several 6" strands of metallic threads. Knot each strand in middle.

20. Fold strands so knot is at top and glue knot to intersection of dowel and star.

21. Stitch dowel to front side of wing. Add small amount of craft glue so dowel cannot be pulled out.

22. Fold tip of wing over, covering stitching. Tack tip of wing to keep in place.

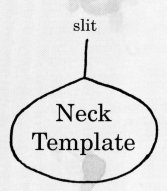

slit

Neck Template

Fairy Goose-Mother's Star
cut 2

open

Greeting the morning with a cheerful tune, Mr. Robin takes time to smell the flowers before going off to play tug-of-war with Mr. Worm.

The Robin's Nest

Materials

- Acrylic paint: black
- Beads: black, 6 mm (2)
- Bird nest
- Cotton print scraps: dk. brown
- Craft glue: white
- Dried moss or excelsior: green
- Embroidery floss: taupe
- Felt scraps: lt. brown; pumpkin
- Floral foam
- Painted terra-cotta pot: 5½"-dia.
- Painted wooden flowers (3–4)
- Polyester stuffing
- Rusty tin (scraps) for wings
- Sprig of silk wild grass
- Upholstery thread: heavy-weight
- Wooden dowel: ¼"-dia. (9")

Tools

- Doll-making needle: long
- Floral wire
- Paintbrush: flat
- Tin snips

Sarah sweeping up the pieces of her broken heart.

Instructions

Refer to Patterns on page 8 before beginning.

1. Using pencil, trace patterns on pages 69–70 onto appropriate fabrics. Trace wing pattern onto tin. Cut out all pieces.

Body

2. With right sides together, stitch body together, leaving openings in back and tail. Clip curves.

3. With right sides together, pin open end of tail together so top and bottom seams match. Stitch across end of tail. Trim seam allowance to ⅛". Turn body right side out.

4. Insert a small amount of polyester stuffing into tail and topstitch tail four times in parallel stitches from end of tail to body. See Diagram A. *Note: Each length of topstitching will be about 1½" long.*

Diagram A

5. Continue stuffing robin until body is very firm. Carefully hand-stitch opening closed.

Beak

6. Stitch felt beak pieces together. Trim to a very narrow seam allowance. Turn beak right side out.

7. Pull felt beak over beak area on robin's face as much as possible. Stitch beak to robin's head. See Diagram B.

Diagram B

Breast

8. With right sides together, pin breast pieces together and stitch. Trim seam allowance close to stitching. Turn right side out. Place on robin's lower body. Pull and smooth out felt, matching lower body seams as indicated on pattern.

9. See Feather Stitch on page 9. Feather-stitch felt to body with taupe embroidery floss.

open

Robin's Body
cut 2

Dowel

open

Robin's Beak
cut 2

Face

10. Using doll-making needle, knot upholstery thread at one end. Make small stitch in eye area.

11. Stitch one bead to each side of head, taking needle back and forth through head and pulling thread slightly to indent eye area. See Diagram C. Make small knot next to bead and bury thread in head. Clip thread at exit point.

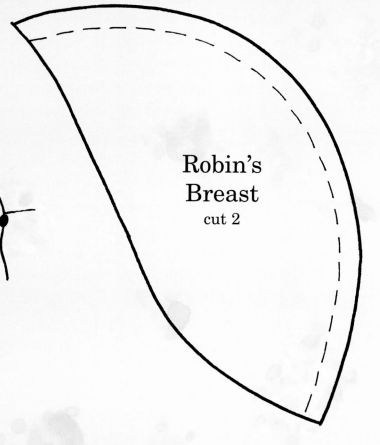

Robin's Breast
cut 2

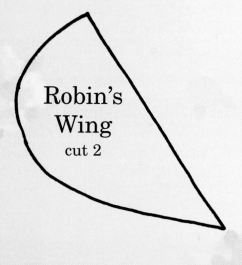

Diagram C

Robin's Wing
cut 2

Wings

12. Using tin snips, cut wings below from rusty tin. Glue wings to robin's body.

13. Using flat paintbrush, paint dowel with black paint. Clip a very small hole for dowel as indicated on pattern. Push dowel inside. *Note: It may help to first sharpen end of dowel in pencil sharpener.*

14. Remove dowel, insert a small amount of craft glue into hole, and insert dowel. Let glue dry for several hours.

Pot

15. Using floral wire, trim foam to fit inside pot. Add a small amount of excelsior to cover top of foam.

16. Place bird nest in middle of pot. Insert stems of wood flowers into sides of nest and foam to hold in place. Push dowel with robin through nest and into foam.

17. Place grass sprig behind robin.

Optional:
The pot and flowers can be hand-painted.

Motifs found in fabric or pictures from magazines can be adhered.

Crackle medium can be applied to the pot.

Jonah's Whale

- Accessories as desired (optional)
- Acrylic paints: black; dk. brown; dolphin gray; dk. green; ivory; lt. ivory; pink blush; mustard yellow
- Color float (a floating additive for paint)
- Crackle medium
- Craft glue: white
- Gel stain: oak
- Polyester stuffing
- Muslin scraps: good quality
- Spray sealer: matte
- Wooden block: 5"-square
- Wooden dowel: ⅜"-dia. (7½")

- Drill/drill bit: ⅜"
- Paintbrushes: flat; liner; small stencil
- Pencil sharpener
- Sanding pad: fine-grit

Jonah's Whale Body
(front)

tape to back pattern piece

Instructions

Refer to Patterns on page 8 before beginning. *Note: Tape pattern pieces together as indicated before tracing pattern onto fabric.*

1. Using pencil, trace patterns on pages 72–74 onto doubled muslin. Cut out all pieces.

Body & Fins

2. Stitch along pencil lines for whale body and fins, leaving an opening at bottom of body and top ends of fins as indicated on pattern.

3. Trim seam allowance to ⅛", clip curves, and turn body right side out.

4. Insert a small amount of polyester stuffing into tail, then topstitch tail as indicated. See Diagram A.

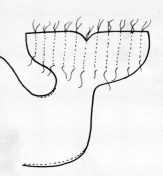

Diagram A

5. Continue, stuffing body firmly. Stitch opening closed, leaving a hole large enough for dowel.

6. Turn fins right side out and press. Press ⅛" seam allowance at opening toward inside of fins. Stitch opening closed.

tape to front pattern piece

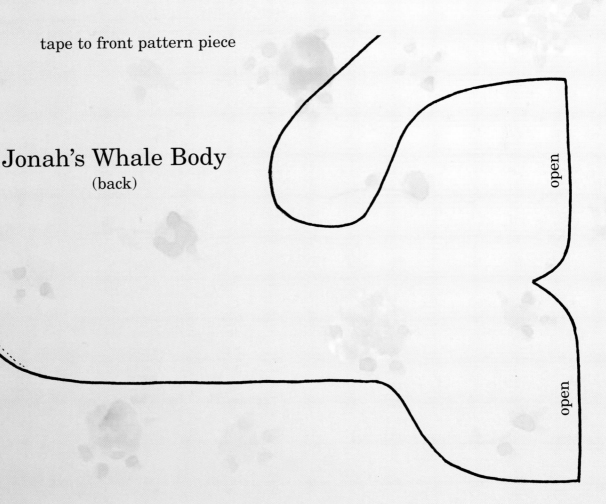

Jonah's Whale Body
(back)

open

open

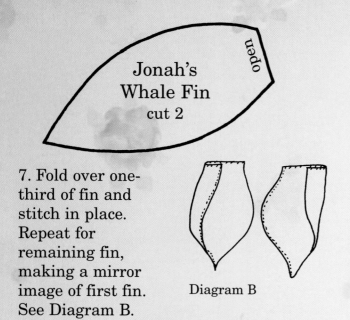

Jonah's Whale Fin
cut 2

open

7. Fold over one-third of fin and stitch in place. Repeat for remaining fin, making a mirror image of first fin. See Diagram B.

Diagram B

8. Stitch fins to whale's body, checking pattern for placement. *Note: The folded edge of fin will be on top.*

Stand

9. Using pencil sharpener, slightly sharpen dowel. Push dowel inside whale belly, working up into stuffing so it is even. Remove dowel. Using flat paintbrush, paint dowel with dk. brown paint. Let dry.

10. Pour a small amount of glue into opening, and insert dowel. See Diagram C. Let dry for several hours.

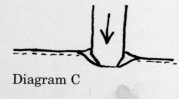

Diagram C

11. Drill hole in center of 5" wooden block to accommodate dowel. Sand wood lightly. Using flat paintbrush, apply two coats of dk. brown paint. Let dry.

12. See Dry-brushing on page 10. Using stencil paintbrush, dry-brush stand with mustard yellow paint. Use a little more paint than typical dry-brush method, especially on corners of stand.

13. Spray stand with sealer. *Note: Do not glue the dowel into the stand yet. You may*

find it easier to hold the dowel in your hand while you paint the whale, then you can place the dowel in the stand during drying time.

14. Base-coat entire whale and fins with dolphin gray paint. Let dry, then apply one or two more coats. *Note: The more coats of paint, the better the whale will crackle.* Let dry.

15. See Floating on page 10. Using flat paintbrush, float ivory paint on whale's belly. *Note: If done correctly, the paint will be quite prominent in center of body, gradually fading to gray color of whale's body.*

Face

16. Using liner paintbrush, paint teeth with lt. ivory paint.

17. Using stencil paintbrush, dry-brush cheek area with pink blush paint. Paint small area at front of mouth with pink blush paint.

18. Using liner paintbrush, paint iris of eye with the dk. green paint, then pupil with black paint. Apply lt. ivory paint to white areas of eye, and a small dot in upper right side of pupil for a highlight.

19. Add a small amount of water to black paint. Using liner paintbrush, paint upper eye line and lashes. Add a small amount of brown paint to black paint and water mixture. Paint mouth outline and very delicate lines for individual teeth. Let dry.

20. Apply crackle medium to painted surfaces of whale, following manufacturer's instructions. Apply gel stain to painted surfaces of whale. Let dry. Spray painted surfaces of whale with sealer.

21. Pour a small amount of glue into stand opening and insert dowel. Let dry for several hours.

Optional:
Glue on accessories as desired.

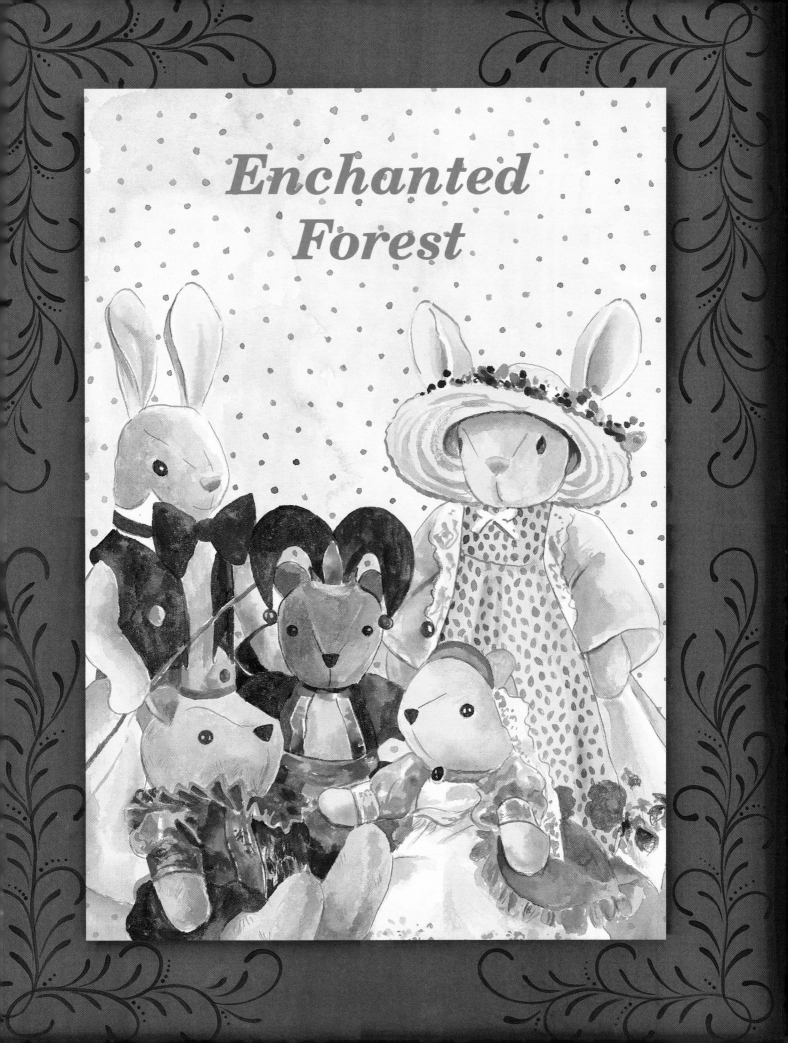

Enchanted Forest

What a wonderful summer! Near the house where they lived, there was a wood. In the long June evenings they liked to go there after tea to bask in the warm sunlight and sit in the cool grass along the riverbank.

Old Felt Bunny

Materials (for one bunny)

- Buttons: resin, ¾" (2); wooden, ¾", painted and lightly sanded (2)
- Cotton fabric scrap for ear linings: print or solid
- Embroidery floss: pale pink
- Plush felt: rabbit color as desired (1 yd.)
- Polyester stuffing (lg. bag)
- Upholstery thread

Tools

- Hot-glue gun/glue sticks
- Sculpting needle: 6"

Instructions for Old Felt Bunny

Refer to Patterns on page 8 before beginning. *Note: Tape pattern pieces together as indicated before tracing pattern onto fabric.*

1. Using pencil, trace patterns on pages 77–82 onto appropriate fabrics. Cut out all pieces.

Ears

2. With right sides together, stitch around each ear, leaving bottom open. Clip curves. Turn right side out. Press lightly on cotton side. Turn open end in ¼" and hand-stitch. Set ears aside.

Old Felt Bunny's
Body
(top)
cut 2

tape to bottom pattern piece

Body

3. With right sides together, pin gusset piece to body piece, matching circles on gusset to nose area on body piece. Stitch, easing in felt if necessary. Pin remaining body piece to gusset and stitch, leaving 4" opening in middle of back seam. See Diagram A.

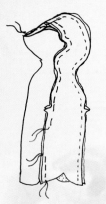

Diagram A

4. Stitch front seam, from nose area down to curved area at bottom of body. Clip at neck. Turn body right side out through back seam opening. Stuff body firmly. Set body aside.

Arms & Legs

5. Place arm pieces with right sides together and stitch around entire arm, leaving an opening as indicated on pattern. Turn right side out. Repeat with remaining arm. Stuff paw and lower arm areas very firmly, but upper arms a little lighter. Stitch openings closed. Set arms aside.

6. Place leg pieces with right sides together and stitch

tape to top pattern piece

Old Felt Bunny's Body
(bottom)
cut 2

Forrest collects the honey.

around entire leg. Repeat for remaining leg. Place stitched legs on a table so backs of legs are next to each other, with feet facing out in opposite directions. Cut 2" slit through one layer of felt in each leg. See Diagram B. Trim seam allowance and clip curves. Turn each foot right side out. Stuff firmly, and stitch openings closed. Set legs aside.

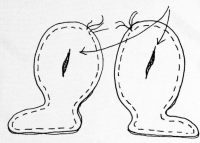

Diagram B

Face

7. See Satin Stitch on page 9. Using sculpting needle, satin-stitch inverted triangle shape for nose with embroidery floss. See Diagram C.

Diagram C

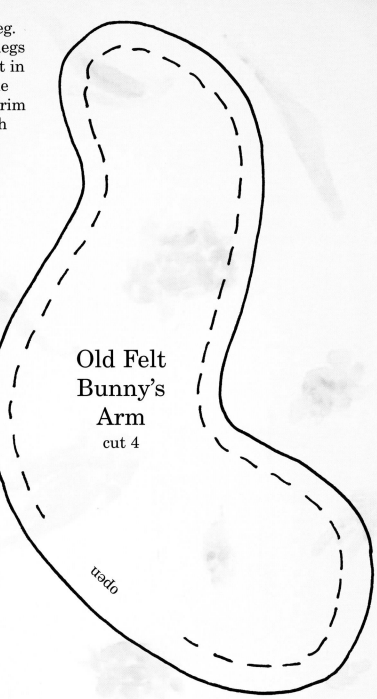

Old Felt Bunny's Arm
cut 4

open

8. Thread sculpting needle with upholstery thread, double thread, and knot. Bring needle up through bottom of wooden button, then back down through opposite hole, bringing needle through two pieces of thread to secure. *Note: The button will now be on end of knotted thread.*

9. Push needle through head in right eye area, through head, and out left eye area. *Note: While needle is through the head, check to make certain the eyes are even.*

10. Bring needle up through bottom of remaining button, back down through opposite hole, back through rabbit's head, and out opposite side through first button. Repeat, going back and forth three or four times, pulling thread a little to indent button eyes slightly.

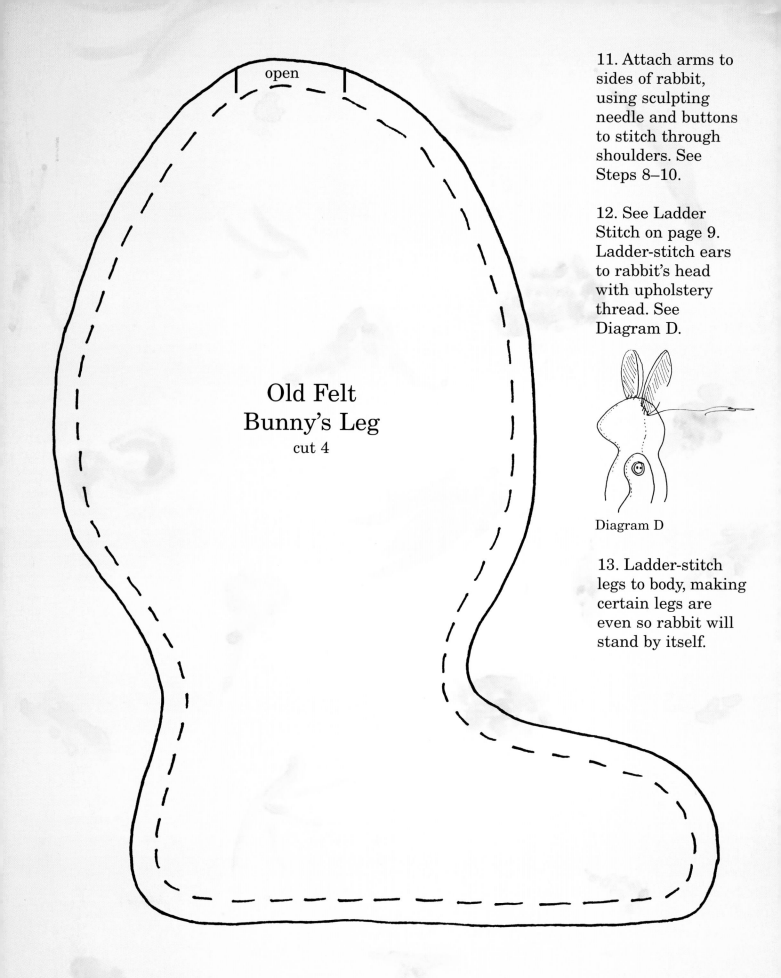

open

Old Felt Bunny's Leg

cut 4

11. Attach arms to sides of rabbit, using sculpting needle and buttons to stitch through shoulders. See Steps 8–10.

12. See Ladder Stitch on page 9. Ladder-stitch ears to rabbit's head with upholstery thread. See Diagram D.

Diagram D

13. Ladder-stitch legs to body, making certain legs are even so rabbit will stand by itself.

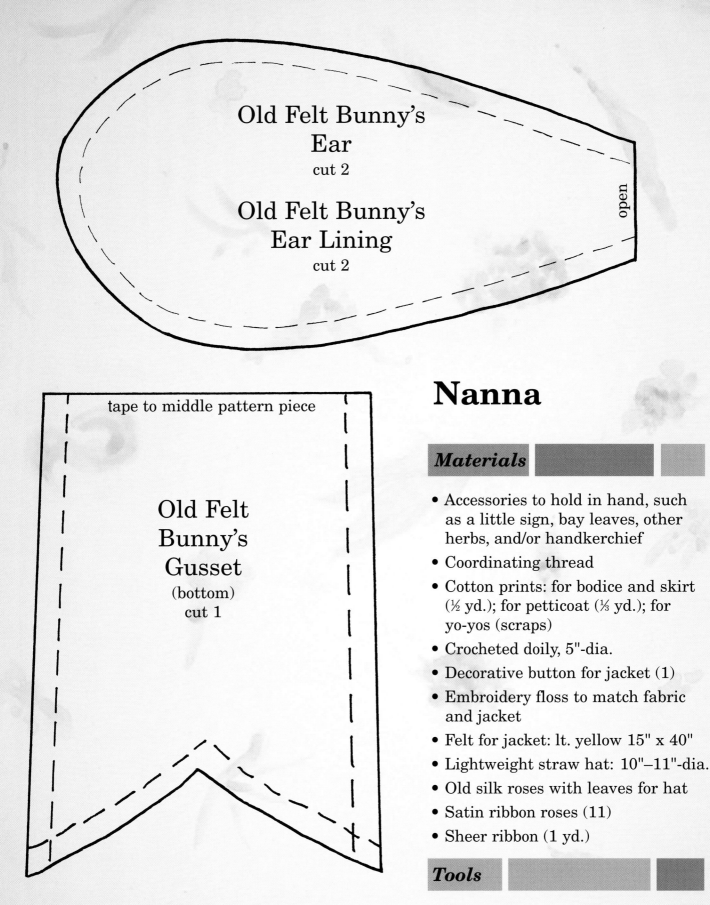

Old Felt Bunny's
Ear
cut 2

Old Felt Bunny's
Ear Lining
cut 2

open

tape to middle pattern piece

Old Felt
Bunny's
Gusset

(bottom)
cut 1

Nanna

Materials

- Accessories to hold in hand, such as a little sign, bay leaves, other herbs, and/or handkerchief
- Coordinating thread
- Cotton prints: for bodice and skirt (½ yd.); for petticoat (⅛ yd.); for yo-yos (scraps)
- Crocheted doily, 5"-dia.
- Decorative button for jacket (1)
- Embroidery floss to match fabric and jacket
- Felt for jacket: lt. yellow 15" x 40"
- Lightweight straw hat: 10"–11"-dia.
- Old silk roses with leaves for hat
- Satin ribbon roses (11)
- Sheer ribbon (1 yd.)

Tools

- Embroidery needle
- Hot-glue gun/glue sticks

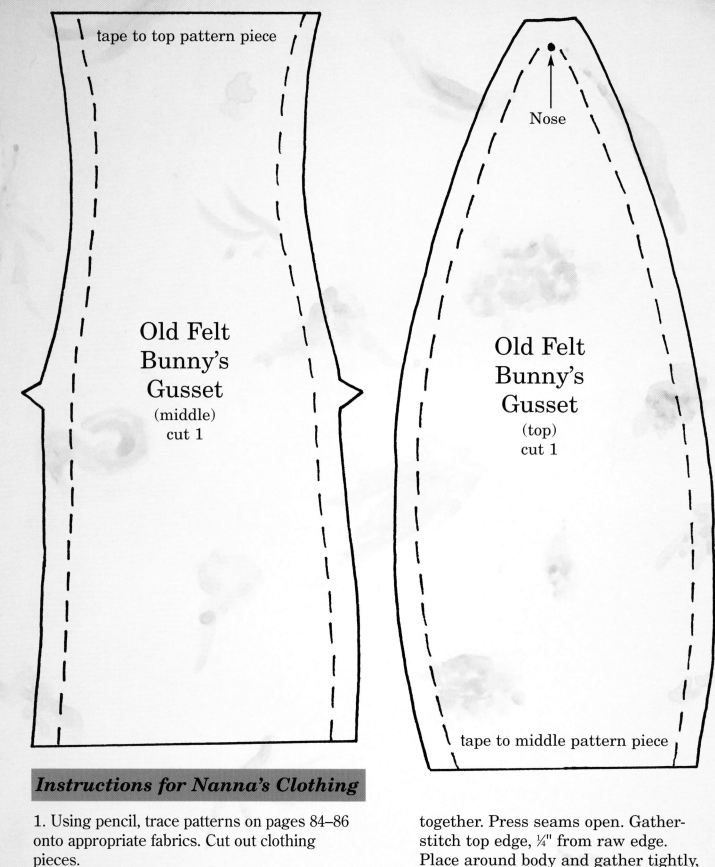

Old Felt Bunny's Gusset (middle) cut 1

tape to top pattern piece

Old Felt Bunny's Gusset (top) cut 1

Nose

tape to middle pattern piece

Instructions for Nanna's Clothing

1. Using pencil, trace patterns on pages 84–86 onto appropriate fabrics. Cut out clothing pieces.

Petticoat

2. Tear 12" x 45" piece from fabric. With right sides together, stitch two 12" edges together. Press seams open. Gather-stitch top edge, ¼" from raw edge. Place around body and gather tightly, just under arms. Apply a little hot glue under gathers to keep petticoat in place.

Bodice

3. With right sides together, stitch front and back pieces at shoulder seams. Press seams open.

4. Cut 1½" x 12" piece from fabric on bias for neck opening. Fold bias piece lengthwise and press.

5. Pin bias piece to right side of fabric at neck opening, matching all raw edges. Stitch ¼" from edge, See Diagram A.

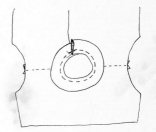

Diagram A

6. Press raw edges toward bodice. With right sides together, stitch side seams. See Diagram B.

Diagram B

Skirt

7. Tear 10¾" x 45" piece from fabric. Press.

8. Gather-stitch skirt to fit lower edge of bodice. With right sides together, stitch bodice to skirt. Press seam toward bodice.

9. With right sides together, stitch back seam of skirt up to within 2" from bodice. Press seam open, turn dress right side out and place on bunny. Hand-stitch remainder of back seam.

10. Cut eight 4" circles. Gather-stitch around edge of circles. Pull thread tightly to gather edges, making yo-yos. Place raw edges inside yo-yos. See Diagram C. Hot-glue one ribbon rose in center of each yo-yo. Hot-glue yo-yos around perimeter of skirt.

Diagram C

Jacket

11. With right sides together, place front and back pieces of vest together and stitch shoulder seams. See Diagram D.

Diagram D

12. With right sides together, pin upper edge of sleeves to arm holes and stitch.

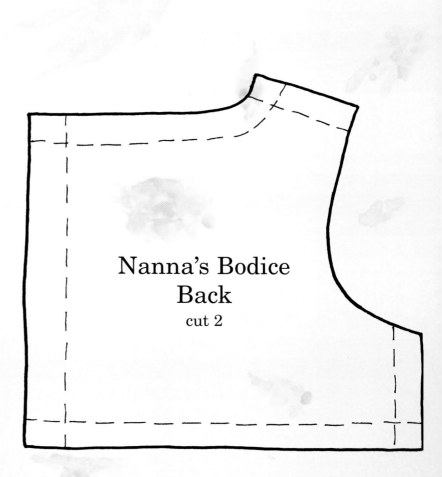

Nanna's Bodice
Front
cut 1

place on fold

Nanna's Bodice
Back
cut 2

13. With right sides together, pin jacket sides to underarm seam and stitch. Trim all edges at each seam so they are even. See Diagram E.

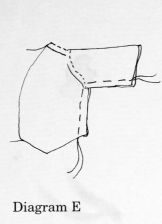

Diagram E

14. See Buttonhole Stitch on page 9. Using embroidery needle, buttonhole-stitch on bottom edge of jacket sleeves and around outside of jacket opening with embroidery floss. See Diagram F.

Diagram F

15. Cut doily in half and stitch to inside edge of jacket, ½" below shoulder seam to midway down jacket opening. See Diagram G. *Note: This will look like a lace lapel.*

Diagram G

16. Stitch button onto front bottom left of jacket.

17. Cut one 2" slit on each side of straw hat for bunny's ears to go through. Hot-glue silk roses with leaves onto straw hat.

18. Tie ribbon into bow. Trim ties in an inverted-V shape. Hot-glue onto back of hat as shown in photograph at right.

Nanna's Jacket
Front
cut 2

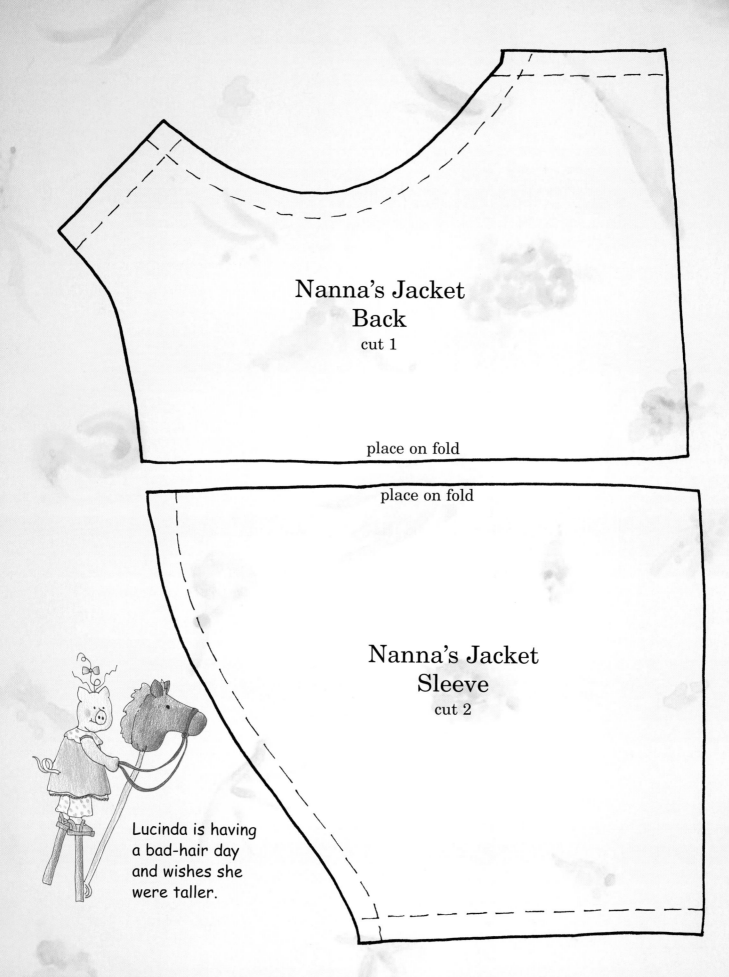

Nanna's Jacket
Back
cut 1

place on fold

place on fold

Nanna's Jacket
Sleeve
cut 2

Lucinda is having
a bad-hair day
and wishes she
were taller.

Mikey

Materials

- Acrylic paint: white
- Cardboard: 4"-square
- Dried moss: green
- Embroidery floss to contrast with vest
- Fabric scrap for tie
- Felt scraps: green for vest; white for collar
- Fishing lures, etc. (optional)
- Leather scraps
- Safety pin
- String
- Tin bucket
- Wooden branch: small
- Yarn: thick (2 yds.)

Tools

- Embroidery needle
- Hot-glue gun/glue sticks
- Paintbrush: liner

Instructions for Mikey's Clothing

1. Using pencil, trace patterns on pages 88–89 onto appropriate fabrics. Cut out clothing pieces.

Vest

2. With right sides together, stitch vest shoulder seams and side seams. Trim seam allowance.

3. See Buttonhole
Stitch on page 9.
Using embroidery
needle, buttonhole-
stitch along outside
edges and sleeve
openings with
embroidery floss.
See Diagram A.

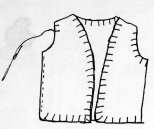

Diagram A

4. Embellish vest with
pocket-shaped patches
of leather. See Dia-
gram B. *Optional:
Fishing lures can be
stitched on the vest,
but make certain this
cannot be reached by
children.*

Diagram B

place on
fold

Mikey's Collar
cut 1

Mikey's Vest
Front
cut 2

Carol's fingernail
polish always takes
forever to dry.

Collar

5. Place collar around bunny's neck, overlapping ends ½". Trim away any excess felt.

6. Stitch ends together in back.

Bow Tie

7. Cut 15" x 1½" piece from fabric. Fold fabric lengthwise and stitch along entire length. Turn right side out. Press.

8. Place tie band on bunny, over collar, overlapping raw ends in front. Stitch together in front. Cut and save excess tubing.

9. Cut two 4" x 5" pieces from same fabric and place right sides together. Stitch around entire rectangle. Cut slit in middle of rectangle, being careful not to cut through both layers of fabric. See Diagram C. Turn right side out through slit and press.

Diagram C

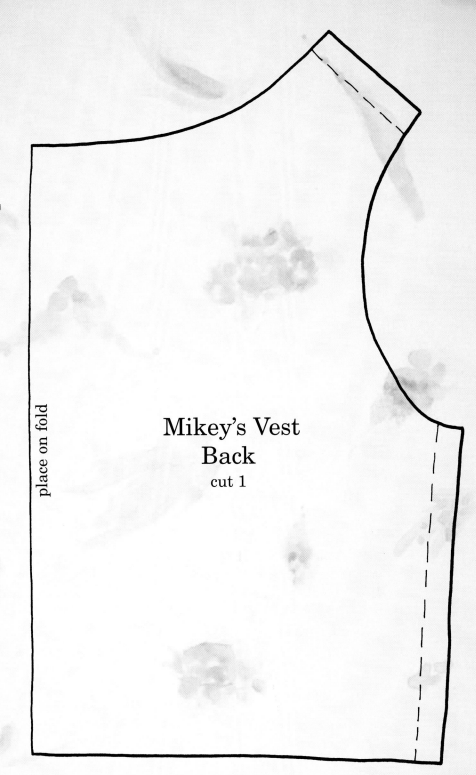

place on fold

Mikey's Vest
Back
cut 1

10. Gather-stitch center of rectangle in bow-tie shape. See Diagram D.

Diagram D

11. Wrap saved piece of tubing around center of bow tie and hot-glue or stitch in back. See Diagram E. Hot-glue bow tie to front of bunny's neck, covering previous stitching.

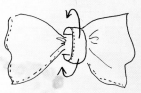

Diagram E

Tail

12. Wind yarn around cardboard piece. Slide yarn off cardboard and tie a piece of yarn around center.

13. Cut all ends. Fluff yarn, creating a tail as shown in photograph at left. Hot-glue center of tail to back of bunny.

Embellishments

14. Using liner paintbrush, print "Worms" on side of tin can in child-like writing with white paint.

15. Stuff can with moss and drape handle over bunny's arm.

16. Make fishing pole from branch and piece of string. Tie safety pin to one end of string for 'hook.' Stitch pole to bunny's paw.

Renaissance Teddy Bear

- Felt scrap for nose: black (optional)
- Polyester stuffing
- Safety eyes and nose: teddy bear
- Shaggy plush felt: craft panels (½ yd.)

Refer to Patterns on page 8 before beginning.

1. Using pencil, trace patterns on pages 92–96 onto appropriate fabrics. Cut out all pieces.

Head

2. With right sides together, match nose dot on gusset and one head piece. Pin pieces together and stitch. Repeat for remaining head piece. See Diagram A.

Diagram A

ear

eye

Renaissance Teddy Bear's
Head
cut 2

open

3. Stitch seam from nose down to front neckline.

4. Using straight pin, mark eye area. Cut tiny X. Insert stem of eye into head.

5. Secure eye in place by pushing metal or plastic disc up stem next to wrong side of fur. Repeat for other eye and nose.

Optional:
Stitch two felt nose pieces together, make slit in one side of felt, and turn nose right side out through slit. Stitch nose to bear's face with matching thread.

Renaissance Teddy Bear's Gusset
cut 1

Optional
Renaissance Teddy Bear's Nose
cut 1

Arms & Body

6. With right sides together, stitch arms, leaving back and top openings unstitched. Turn arms right side out. Set arms aside.

7. With right sides together, stitch front body pieces together at center front. See Diagram B.

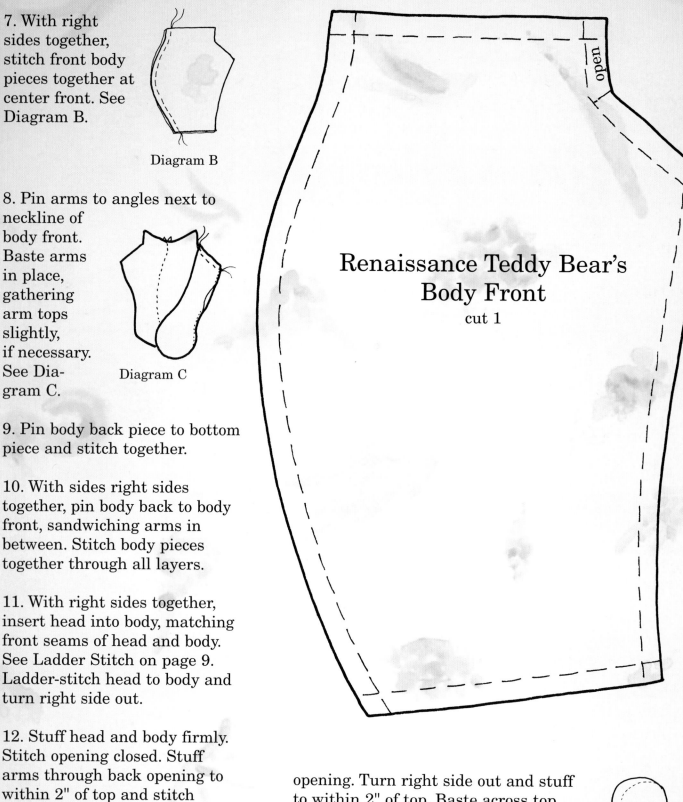

Diagram B

8. Pin arms to angles next to neckline of body front. Baste arms in place, gathering arm tops slightly, if necessary. See Diagram C.

Diagram C

9. Pin body back piece to bottom piece and stitch together.

10. With sides right sides together, pin body back to body front, sandwiching arms in between. Stitch body pieces together through all layers.

11. With right sides together, insert head into body, matching front seams of head and body. See Ladder Stitch on page 9. Ladder-stitch head to body and turn right side out.

12. Stuff head and body firmly. Stitch opening closed. Stuff arms through back opening to within 2" of top and stitch opening closed.

Legs

13. With right sides together, stitch around legs, leaving

opening. Turn right side out and stuff to within 2" of top. Baste across top opening, matching front and back seams.

14. With toes pointing toward nose, pin legs to bottom edge of body front. Ladder-stitch legs to body. See Diagram D.

Diagram D

Renaissance Teddy Bear's Body Front
cut 1

open

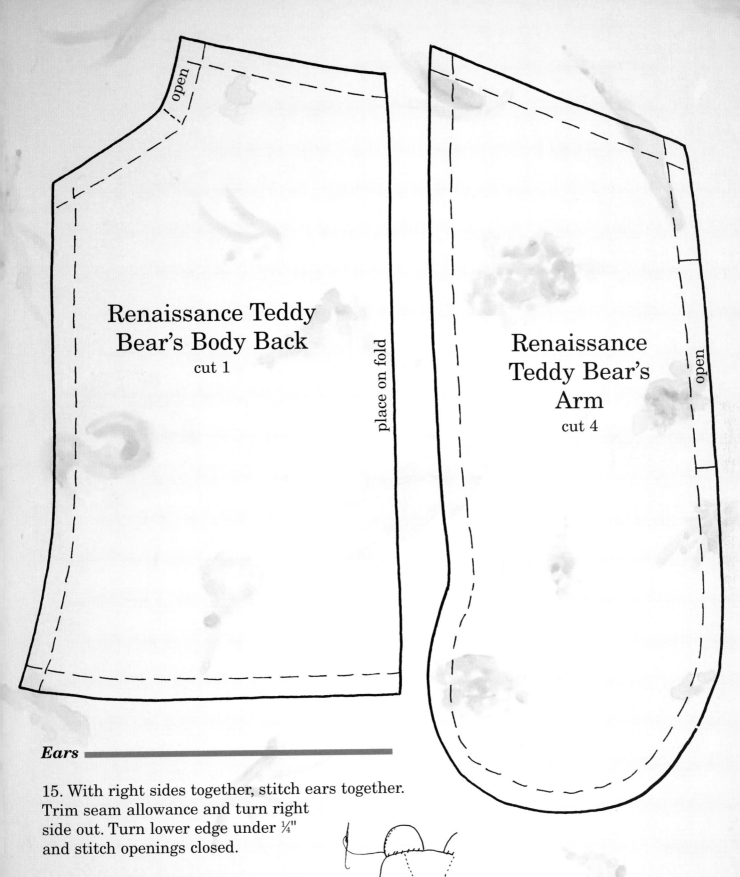

Renaissance Teddy Bear's Body Back
cut 1

open

place on fold

Renaissance Teddy Bear's Arm
cut 4

open

Ears

15. With right sides together, stitch ears together. Trim seam allowance and turn right side out. Turn lower edge under ¼" and stitch openings closed.

16. Pin ears to bear's head, straddling seam of gusset and head pieces. Stitch ears in place. See Diagram E.

Diagram E

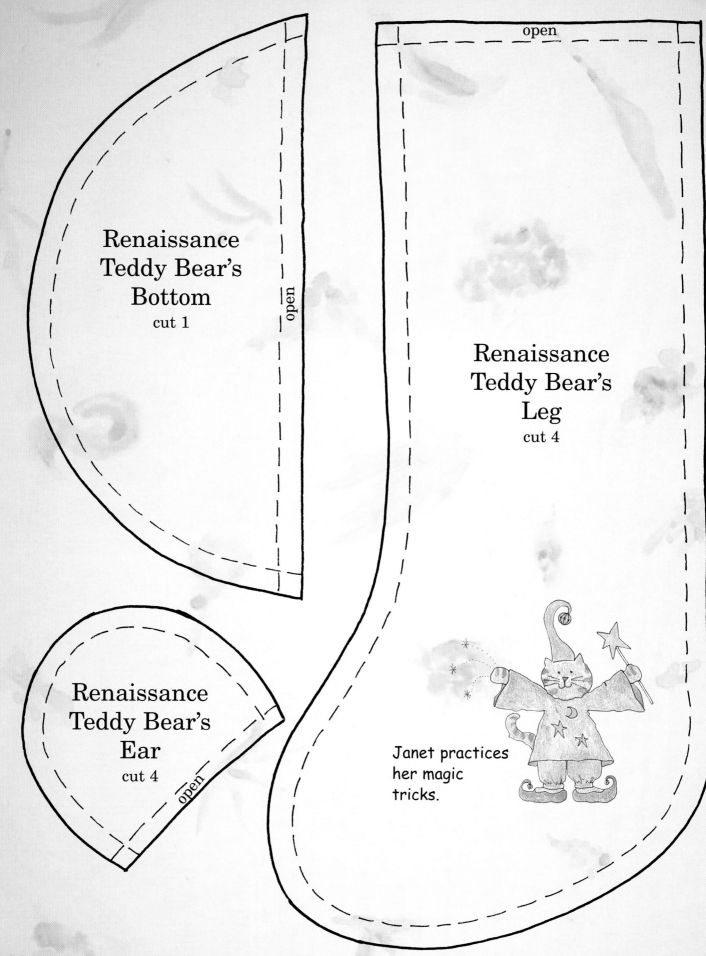

Renaissance
Teddy Bear's
Bottom
cut 1

open

open

Renaissance
Teddy Bear's
Leg
cut 4

Renaissance
Teddy Bear's
Ear
cut 4

open

Janet practices
her magic
tricks.

It isn't easy being King of the Forest— the meetings, the formal dinners, and the royal soirees. There just isn't ever time for that which is so very important—and that is a nice long nap.

King Tinton

Materials

- Antique gold trim: ½"-wide (¼ yd)
- Brocade fabric for trousers (⅛ yd.)
- Brocade ribbons: 1"-wide (1⅛ yds.); 2½"-wide for sleeve cuffs (½ yd.)
- Decorative jewel-like button
- Embroidery floss to match tunic
- Fabric paint with applicator tip: gold
- Fabrics: scraps for shirt (6" x 8"); for sleeves (⅙ yd.)
- Fringe trim: 1½"-wide (⅔ yd.)
- Muslin scrap for crown
- Satin picot-edged ribbon: ¼"-wide (⅔ yd.)
- Textured paint: metallic gold
- Velvet wired-edged ribbon for ruff: 2½"-wide (2 yds.)

Tools

- Embroidery needle
- Hot-glue gun/glue sticks
- Paintbrushes: flat (2)

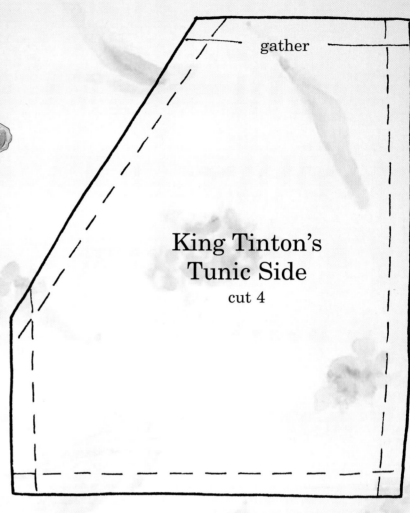

King Tinton's Tunic Side

cut 4

gather

Instructions

1. See Renaissance Teddy Bear on pages 92–96. Create teddy bear.

Instructions for Clothing

1. Using pencil, trace patterns on page 98–101 onto appropriate fabrics. Cut out clothing pieces.

Tunic

2. With right sides together, stitch tunic sides to tunic center front and back. Press seams open.

3. Center 1" piece of satin ribbon over each seam and stitch ribbon along each side.

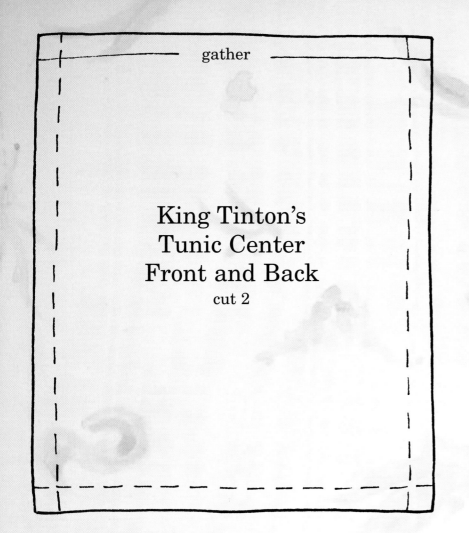

gather

King Tinton's Tunic Center Front and Back

cut 2

9. Using embroidery needle, gather-stitch around neck and sleeves edges with embroidery floss. Gather-stitch around lower edges of sleeves. Place on bear and pull gathers tightly around neck and sleeves. Knot.

10. Stitch 2½"-wide brocade ribbon around lower edges of sleeves, covering gathered edges. Overlap ribbon at back of the bear's arm, folding top edge under ¼". Hot-glue in place. See Diagram C.

Diagram C

4. With right sides together, stitch sleeves to tunic front. See Diagram A.

Diagram A

5. With right sides together, stitch sleeves to tunic back. Press seams open.

6. With right sides together, stitch sides and sleeves. See Diagram B. Clip corners and press seams open. Turn lower edge of sleeve under ⅜". Hand-stitch hem in place.

7. With right sides together, stitch fringe to lower edge of tunic. Press seam allowance toward tunic.

Diagram B

8. Zigzag-stitch satin ribbon to right side of tunic, above fringe. *Note: This will help keep the seam allowance flat.*

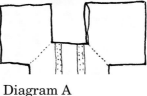

Thursday was a stressful day for Nellie . . .

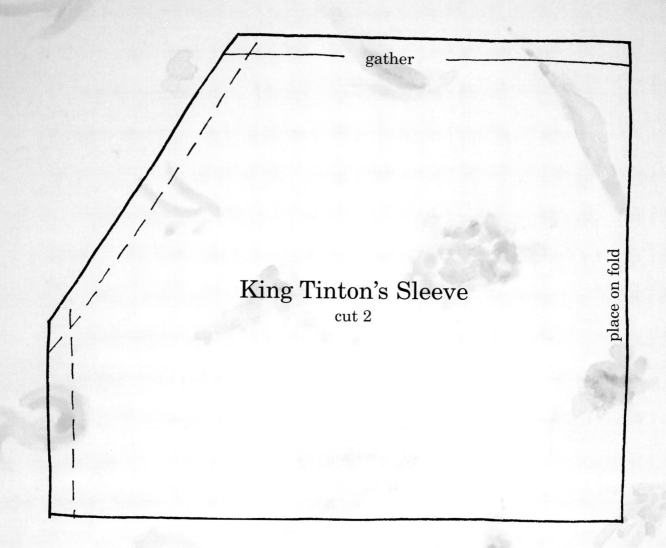

King Tinton's Sleeve
cut 2

gather

place on fold

Trousers

11. Cut two 10" x 22½" pieces from fabric. Cut 3" slit up middle, then stitch sides and inseam. Clip curves. Turn trousers right side out. Press.

12. Using embroidery needle, gather-stitch top and leg openings with embroidery floss. Place trousers on bear. Pull gathers tightly around waist and legs. See Diagram D. Knot.

Diagram D

13. Stitch 1"-wide brocade ribbon around gathered edges of leg openings. Overlap ribbon at back of bear's leg, folding top edge under ¼". Hot-glue in place.

All his friends thought Anthony was real cool.

14. Accordion-pleat entire length of velvet ribbon. See Diagram E. *Note: The pleats are approximately ⅝" wide.* Using embroidery needle and embroidery floss, stitch pleats together at one edge to fit around bear's neck. See Diagram F. Tie floss in knot at back and hot-glue ends of ribbon together.

Diagram E

Diagram F

Crown

15. Stitch muslin together and trim seam allowances. Clip corners. Turn right side out. Hand-stitch edges together, overlapping back edges.

16. Using flat paintbrush, paint crown with textured metallic gold paint and shape so base is circular. Let dry. Hot-glue trim to bottom edge.

17. Using tip of applicator, make small scrolls and dots to decorate the pointed ends of crown with fabric paint. Hot-glue button to front of crown.

18. Using tip of applicator, make small dots outside perimeter of button with fabric paint. Let dry. Hot-glue crown to top of bear's head.

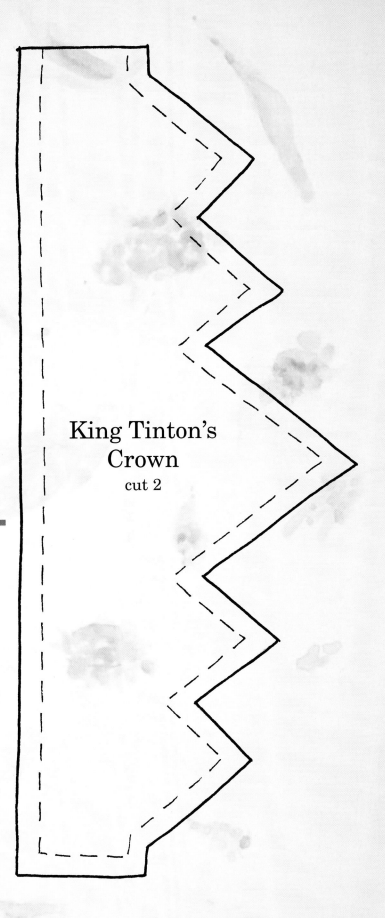

King Tinton's Crown
cut 2

I'm "Queen for the Day" and
what a lovely title that is.
My everyday duties are being
tended to by another while
I'm given the luxury of being
pampered, ears to toes. I
think that I shall be
the queen for
tomorrow, too.

Queen Mindestronie

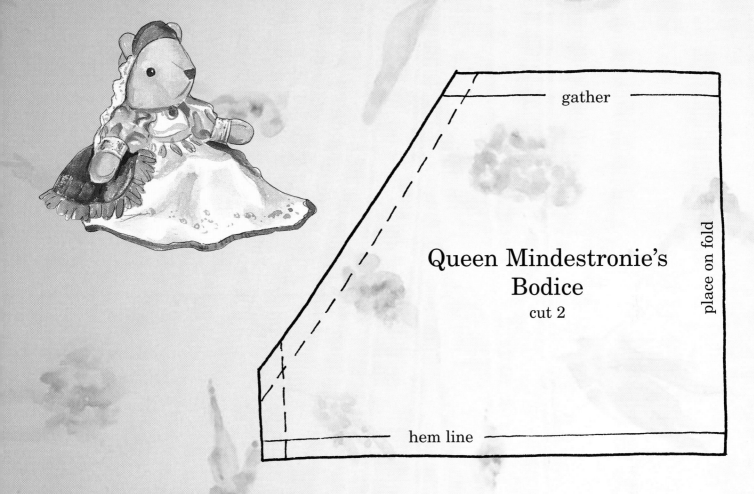

Queen Mindestronie's
Bodice
cut 2

gather

place on fold

hem line

Materials

- Bridal lace: 8"-wide (15")
- Brocade ribbon: gold/white, 1"-wide, (½ yd.)
- Cotton quilt batting scrap: low-loft
- Decorative button
- Embroidery floss to match skirt
- Fabrics: for bodice and skirt (½ yd.); for sleeves (⅙ yd.); for overskirt lining (¼ yd.)
- Lace for bloomers: 1½"-wide (1⅛ yd.)
- Mesh fabric for overskirt: gold (¼ yd.)
- Metallic gold trims: for headpiece (¼ yd.); for neckline and skirt (1⅔ yds.)
- Muslin for bloomers (⅓ yd.)
- Rope-fringe trim for overskirt: 2½"-wide (1⅓ yds.)
- Tasseled trim for bodice (½ yd.)

Tools

- Embroidery needle
- Hot-glue gun/glue sticks

Instructions

1. See Renaissance Teddy Bear on pages 92–96. Create teddy bear.

Instructions for Clothing

1. Using pencil, trace patterns on pages 104–105 onto appropriate fabrics. Cut out clothing pieces.

Note: If you can, find antique linens or old piano scarves with embroidery and crocheted edges that might be an appropriate look for this bear.

Bloomers

2. Cut two 10" x 22½" pieces from fabric. Cut 3" slit up middle, then stitch sides and inseam. Clip curves. Turn bloomers right side out. Press.

3. Zigzag-stitch lower edge of bloomers, then overlap 1½"-wide lace over lower edges. Stitch ends of lace to bloomers, overlapping ends of lace and folding top edge under. See Diagram A. Stitch ends of lace together.

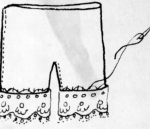

Diagram A

gather

Queen Mindestronie's
Sleeve
cut 2

place on fold

4. Using embroidery needle, gather-stitch top and leg openings above top edge of lace with embroidery floss. Place bloomers on bear, pull gathers tightly and knot ends together.

Skirt

5. Cut 14" x 45" piece from fabric. With right sides together, stitch 14" edges together. Press seam open. Turn skirt right side out. Zigzag-stitch lower edge, if necessary.

6. Stitch trim to lower edge of skirt. Using embroidery needle, gather-stitch top edge of skirt with embroidery floss. See Diagram B. Place skirt on bear with seam in back and top edge under arms. Pull gathers tightly and tie ends of floss in a knot.

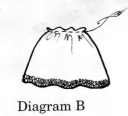

Diagram B

Overskirt

7. Cut 6½" x 36" piece from lining fabric. Round off opposite lower ends of fabric. See Diagram C.

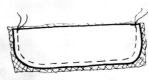

Diagram C

8. With right sides together, pin lining to mesh fabric. Stitch sides, curves, and lower edge of fabrics, then trim edges. *Note: Zigzag-stitch edges if the fabric tends to fray.* Turn right side out and press.

9. Stitch rope trim to underside of lining. See Diagram D. Using embroidery needle, gather-stitch top edge to fit top edge of underskirt with embroidery floss, leaving 4¾" opening in front. Stitch in place over underskirt. See Diagram E.

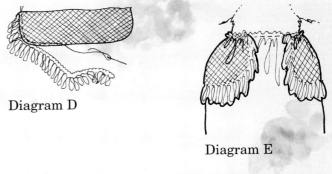

Diagram D

Diagram E

Bodice

10. With right sides together, stitch sleeves to bodice. Press seams open. Zigzag-stitch lower edges of sleeves and bodice.

11. With right sides together, stitch sides and sleeves together. Clip corners. Turn bodice right side out and press.

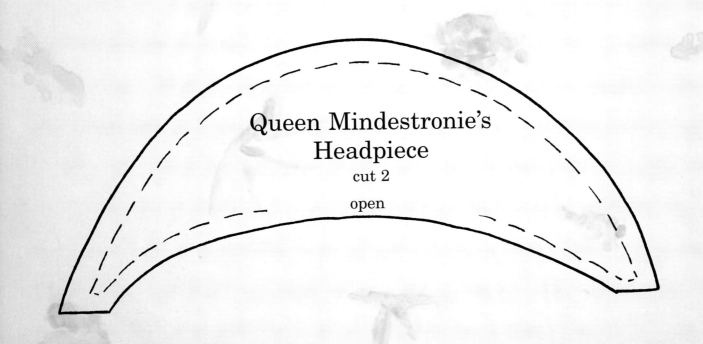

Queen Mindestronie's
Headpiece

cut 2

open

12. Stitch tasseled trim to lower edge of bodice. Using embroidery needle, gather-stitch around edge of neck and sleeve openings with embroidery floss.

13. Place bodice on bear, pull neck and sleeve gathers tightly, and tie ends of floss in a knot.

14. Stitch brocade ribbon around lower edges of sleeve gathers, overlapping ribbon in back, and folding top edge of ribbon under ¼". Hot-glue in place.

15. Stitch gold trim around neck of bear, overlapping ends in back.

16. Stitch button to front center of neck trim.

Headpiece

17. With right sides together, pin headpiece pieces to top of double layers of quilt batting.

18. Stitch headpiece together, leaving an opening for turning as indicated on pattern. Trim seam allowance to ⅛". Clip corners. Turn right side out. Stitch opening closed and press.

19. Hot-glue metallic gold trim to top edge of head-piece, and ends of bridal lace to back side of corners. See Diagram F.

Diagram F

20. Hot-glue headpiece to bear's head, just in front of ears.

Nitworth
the Jester

Materials

- Bells: gold, ¾" (4)
- Decorative button for belt
- Embroidery floss: black
- Fabric prints: black for clothing (⅛ yd.); dk. red for clothing (⅛ yd.); yellow for clothing (scraps)
- Polyester stuffing
- Ribbons: metallic gold, ¾"-wide (1½ yds.); red/gold brocade, 1¼"-wide (⅝ yd.)
- Trims: gold, 1"-wide (1¼ yds); gold/red, 1½"-wide (⅛ yd.)

Tools

- Embroidery needle
- Hot-glue gun/glue sticks

Roger is glad jester school is out for the summer.

Instructions

1. See Renaissance Teddy Bear on pages 92–96. Create teddy bear substituting Jester Leg patterns on pages 111–112 for legs.

2. Using embroidery needle, stitch one bell on tip of each foot with embroidery floss.

Instructions for Clothing

1. Using pencil, trace patterns on page 109–113 onto appropriate fabrics as shown in photograph on page 107. *Note: Tape pattern pieces together as indicated before tracing onto fabric.* Cut out clothing pieces.

Tunic

2. With right sides together, stitch tunic sides to tunic center front and back. Press seams open.

3. Center a piece of metallic gold ribbon over each seam and stitch ribbon along each side. See Diagram A.

Diagram A

4. With right sides together, stitch sleeves to front of tunic.

5. With right sides together, stitch sleeves to back of tunic. Press seams open.

6. Zigzag-stitch along lower edges of the sleeve. Pin metallic gold ribbon ½" above zigzagged edges and stitch along edges of ribbon.

gather

tape to bottom pattern piece

Jester's Tunic Center
Front and Back
(top)
cut 2

7. With right sides together, stitch sides and sleeves. Clip corners and press seams open. Turn lower edge of sleeve under ⅜". Hand-stitch hem in place.

8. Turn tunic right side out and stitch gold trim to lower edge of tunic. *Note: When stitching, form a small dart in the top edge of the trim so it will lie flat when you are finished stitching.*

9. Using embroidery needle, gather-stitch around neck and sleeve edges with embroidery floss. Place tunic on bear, pull floss to gather tightly around bear's neck, and tie in a knot.

tape to top pattern piece

Jester's Tunic Center
Front and Back
(bottom)
cut 2

gather

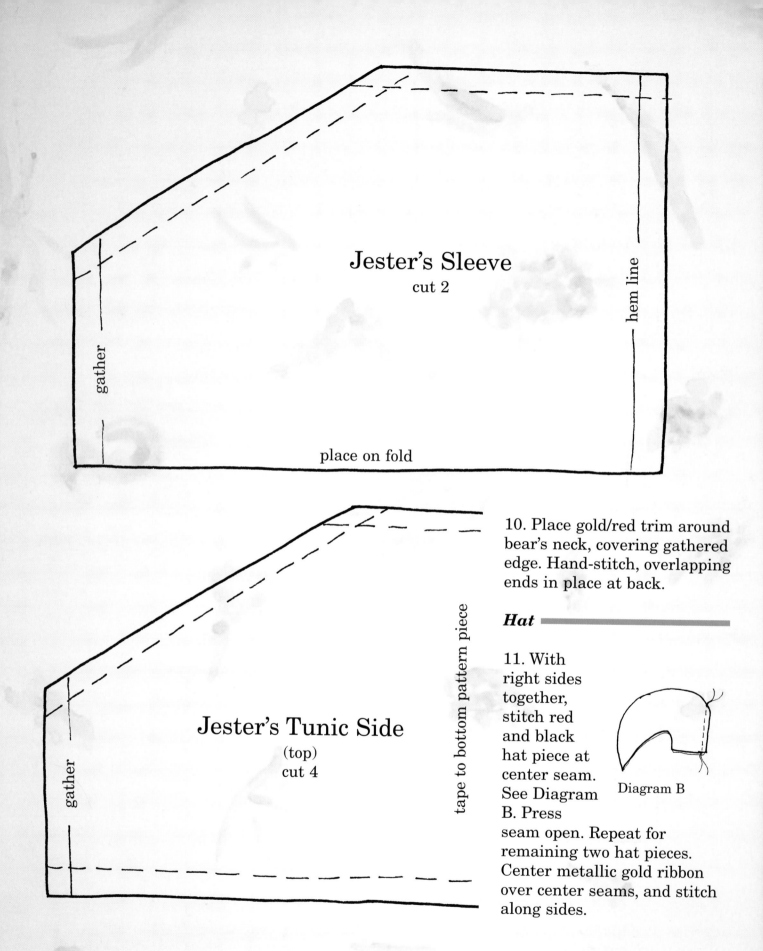

Jester's Sleeve

cut 2

gather

hem line

place on fold

Jester's Tunic Side

(top)
cut 4

gather

tape to bottom pattern piece

10. Place gold/red trim around bear's neck, covering gathered edge. Hand-stitch, overlapping ends in place at back.

Hat

11. With right sides together, stitch red and black hat piece at center seam. See Diagram B. Press seam open. Repeat for remaining two hat pieces. Center metallic gold ribbon over center seams, and stitch along sides.

Diagram B

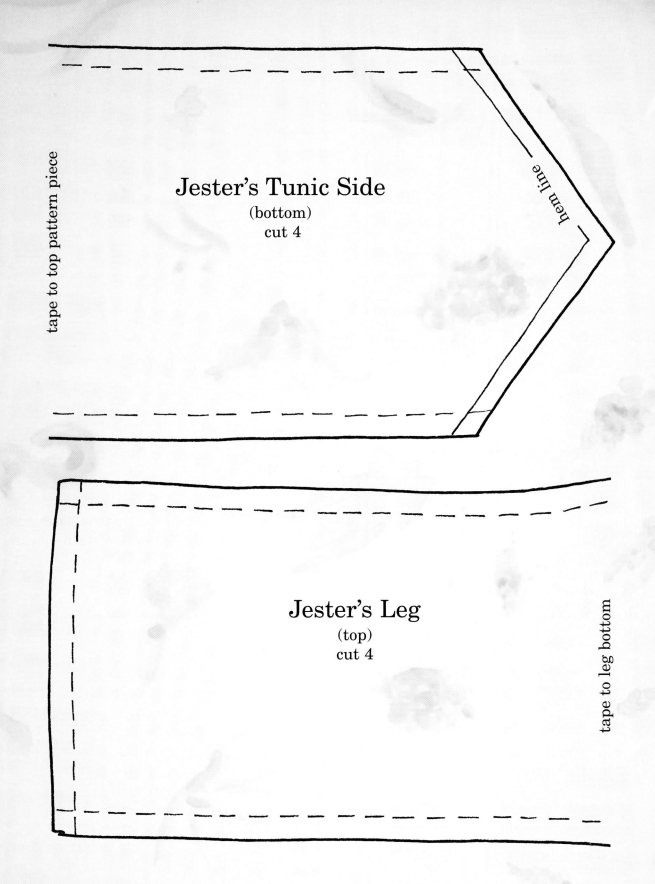

Jester's Tunic Side
(bottom)
cut 4

tape to top pattern piece

hem line

Jester's Leg
(top)
cut 4

tape to leg bottom

12. With right sides together, stitch hat together, leaving lower end open. Clip curves. Turn hat right side out.

13. Cut 2¼" x 6¾" rectangle from scrap fabric for hat band. With right sides together, stitch 2¼" edges together. Press seam open.

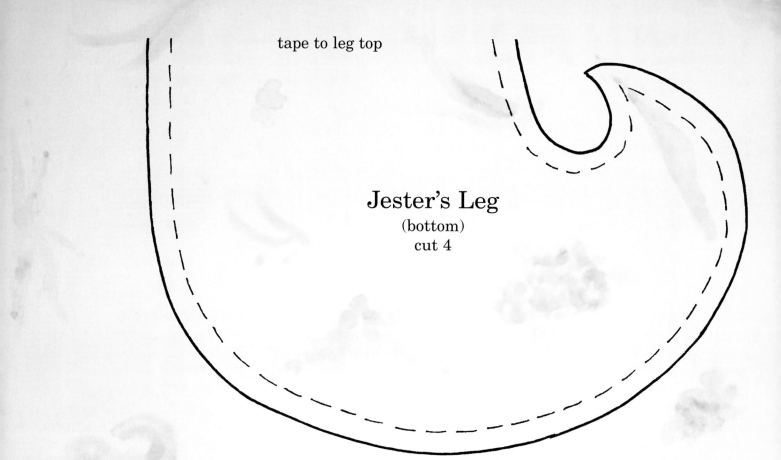

tape to leg top

Jester's Leg
(bottom)
cut 4

14. With wrong sides together, fold band in half lengthwise, matching raw edges. Baste edges together and pin band to hat, matching raw edges, and back seams of hat and band. See Diagram C. Stitch band to hat, then press band down with seam allowance toward hat.

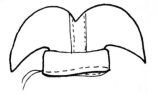

Diagram C

Jester's Hat
cut 4

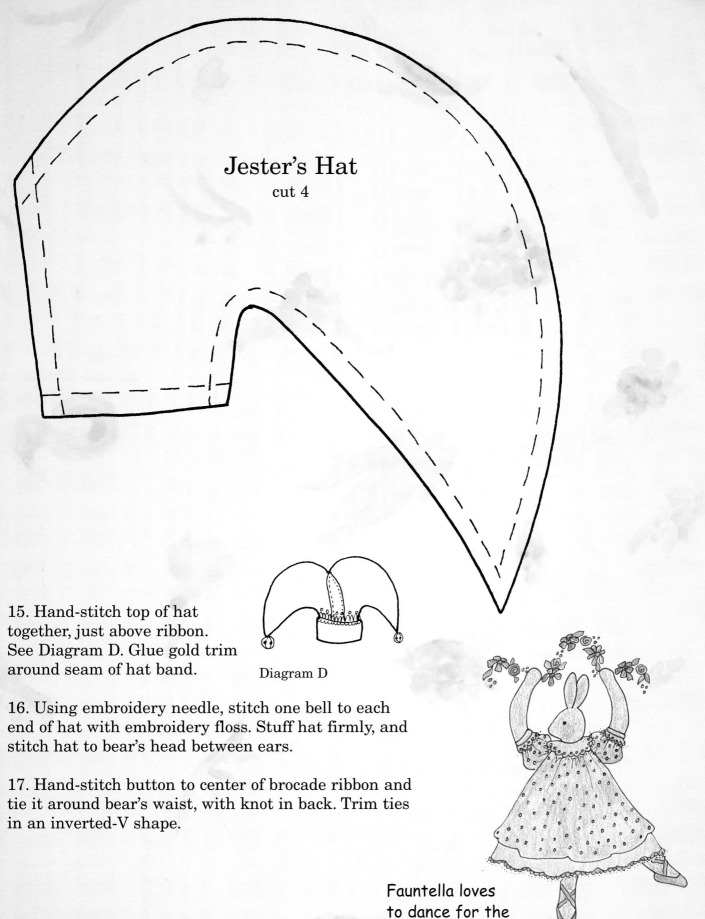

15. Hand-stitch top of hat together, just above ribbon. See Diagram D. Glue gold trim around seam of hat band.

Diagram D

16. Using embroidery needle, stitch one bell to each end of hat with embroidery floss. Stuff hat firmly, and stitch hat to bear's head between ears.

17. Hand-stitch button to center of brocade ribbon and tie it around bear's waist, with knot in back. Trim ties in an inverted-V shape.

Fauntella loves to dance for the royal family.

Gallery

Angelia McLean

Angelia McLean began making teddy bears in 1989, but the world of miniatures has been a part of her since 1971. By combining these two art forms, she was able to begin her career as an international teddy bear artist and contribute her creations to the miniature teddy bear collectible market in 1994.

Angelia's teddy bears average 2½" and under. They are made from synthetic upholstery fabrics, a soft fur-like material and suitable for scale. Their eyes are glass beads and each has hundreds of fine hand-stitches. Each has completely moveable limbs with cotter pin mechanisms. Angelia has the unique ability to breathe "life" into her creations. She prides herself in the fact that even in the tiny size and with such a medium, every teddy bear or animal is unique with its own personality. Angelia devotes a great deal of attention to details. Some of her bears have items such as dresses with buttons, tiny necklaces, eyelashes, eyelids, and silk roses no larger than the head of a pin.

She lives in Denver, Colorado, with her husband Paul, their four children, and a house full of pets.

Melinda Small Paterson

Melinda grew up in Colorado with people who were inventive, messy, and respectful of the mountains in which they played. Her father built scale models and parade floats, and did sculpting. Her mother was a symphony manager and her three brothers are involved in the arts.

In 1980 she began by making dollhouses and miniature furniture, then later taught classes with the National Association of Miniature Enthusiasts. Her miniatures can be seen at the Rosalie Whyel Doll Museum and her porcelain dolls have won Artisan level in the International Guild of Miniature Artisans. Her fairy dolls have won awards at the Santa Fe Doll Art Festival.

Mythology and folklore have been the source of images for her current interest in producing cloth dolls, animals and patterns. Dolls are the best way for her to combine all her favorite things: drawing, painting, sculpting, beading, textiles, and teaching.

Pam Gary & Traci Benvegnu

Pam Gary

Traci Benvegnu

Created by Pam Gary

The partnership of Pam Gary and Traci Benvegnu began in a sculpting seminar. The two met and became fast friends. Then they started to cause as much trouble as they could think of. They create dolls together and as individual artists.

After joining forces with each other, Pam and Traci sold their work at the Toy Fair in New York City. They also ran an original doll art show that toured seventeen art galleries and doll stores in Colorado, and featured 22 doll artists. And after being approached by Barbara Campbell, editor of *Soft Dolls and Animals Magazine*, they began designing dolls for articles in the magazine. Their dolls have been featured twice on the cover.

Additionally, they have worked with a crew of artists to create animated window displays for the Downtown Denver Christmas festivities. Currently, the two are working on an animated short film as well as their individual art.

Created by Traci Benvegnu

Etta B. Lewis

Etta B. Lewis never played with dolls, even as a child. Instead she made hats from hollyhock leaves and flowers. She took up doll-making eight years ago and has almost given up any other type of craft or art. Doll-making is a great joy to Etta. It appealed to her because it satisfied her need to costume, going back to those flower and leaf hats she made as a child.

Etta loves to give her animal dolls human traits, but with an animal's arrogance. Her joy is in the doll-making process and she is always excited to begin the next creation.

Muriel Spencer

Muriel's love of animals is reflected in her ability to create lifelike replicas of favorite pets or species in fur fabric. By looking at photographs of a customer's pet, she takes pains to capture the personality of each animal, sculpting with a doll needle and airbrushing the fur.

Muriel helped reestablish a craft co-op for Inuit women in Taloyoak, 200 miles above the Arctic Circle, in Canada's Northwest Territories. She designed the muslin cat, snake, and frog for Jaquard's craft kits, distributed around the world and included in several art catalogs. She also has designed life-sized African animals—a zebra, leopard, and cub—for Fairfield Processing Inc., designed a line of stuffed-animal patterns for her company, Spencer's Zoo, and created several articles for leading craft magazines. Muriel has designed animals for toy companies and taught in the public school system and through workshops.

Akira Blount

Akira Blount was born in Columbus, Ohio, in 1945. She graduated from the University of Wisconsin with a Bachelor's degree in Art Education. In 1970, she started making sock and stocking dolls for her infant son. This activity struck a chord with Akira's past and current love of fabrics and designs. As a child, she spent many hours with her grandmother who taught her to sew clothes for her doll.

Over the next 10 years, she continued making dolls and learning skills required to be a professional craftswoman and doll artist. In 1977, she met her current husband and partner Larry Blount and she joined Southern Highlands Craft Guild, a regional professional craftsman organization, which gave

her a place to market her work and start refining her skills as an artist.

Her work, since the early days in Chicago, has been very well received. She has continually striven to grow and change her designs, fabrics, subject matter, and markets. Her most recent work uses paperclay over cloth.

In 1994, she was nationally recognized by inclusions as one of 70 craft artists in the White House Collection of American Crafts. Her works have been published in numerous books and magazines. She has served on the board of several regional and national organizations and is currently president of the National Institute of American Doll Artists, an international organization dedicated to the art of the doll.

Betts Vidal

A small chalkboard placed 18" from the floor by Betts' parents was their way of encouraging her to draw at the tender age of 18 months. She has no recollection of the little chalkboard, but she cannot remember not drawing. To this day, Betts can sketch a thought easier than she can articulate one. Thanks to her Mom and Dad.

Betts' first introduction to sewing was at her first Brownie meeting. Her patient leader taught her to

thread and knot a needle by winding it around her index finger, rolling it, then removing it with the help of a fingernail . . . at the age of seven, she thought . . . "The world is mine!" From that point on, she envisioned herself transforming fabrics into anything a doll, her younger sisters, or she could wear. Treasured snippets of these long ago fabrics are reminders of her earlier attempts.

Dolls, dolls, dolls, will be a lifelong way of incorporating all Betts has experienced into a most rewarding form of creativity. The dolls have taken her to many new places, other countries, and to treasured friendships. Best of all, her husband, children, grandchildren, siblings, and parents all share in her delight of dolls.

Acknowledgments

We would like to offer our sincere appreciation for the valuable support given in this ever-changing industry of new ideas, concepts, designs, and products. Several projects shown in this publication were created with outstanding and innovative products developed by All Cooped Up, Hollywood Trims-Dritz, Rosebar Fabrics, C.M. Offray & Son, Kunin Felt, Americana Acrylic Paints, and Delta Ceramcoat® Acrylic Paints.

Abijah Montgomery III
Americana Acrylic Paints:
Delane's Dark Flesh
Driftwood
Ebony Black
Graphite
Light Buttermilk
Mississippi Mud
Slate Grey

Fairy Goose-Mother
Americana Acrylic Paint:
Raspberry
Delta Ceramcoat® Acrylic Paint:
Light Gold

Jonah's Whale
Delta Ceramcoat® Acrylic Paints:
Black
Dark Brown
Dolphin Gray
Ivory
Light Ivory
Olive Yellow
Pink Blush
Salem Green

Mephisto the Lion
Americana Acrylic Paints:
Bittersweet Chocolate
Golden Straw
Lamp Black
Light Buttermilk
Shading Flesh

Miss Anne
Delta Ceramcoat® Acrylic Paints:
Cadet Gray
Caucasian Flesh

Miss Ruth
Delta Ceramcoat® Acrylic Paints:
Burnt Umber
Caucasian Flesh
Golden Brown

Red Hen & Cocky Le Doodle
Delta Ceramcoat® Acrylic Paints:
Black
Lichen Grey
Moroccan Red
Pigskin
Storm Grey

Conversion Chart

mm-millimetres cm-centimetres
inches to millimetres and centimetres

inches	mm	cm	inches	cm	inches	cm
⅛	3	0.3	9	22.9	30	76.2
¼	6	0.6	10	25.4	31	78.7
⅜	10	1.0	11	27.9	32	81.3
½	13	1.3	12	30.5	33	83.8
⅝	16	1.6	13	33.0	34	86.4
¾	19	1.9	14	35.6	35	88.9
⅞	22	2.2	15	38.1	36	91.4
1	25	2.5	16	40.6	37	94.0
1¼	32	3.2	17	43.2	38	96.5
1½	38	3.8	18	45.7	39	99.1
1¾	44	4.4	19	48.3	40	101.6
2	51	5.1	20	50.8	41	104.1
2½	64	6.4	21	53.3	42	106.7
3	76	7.6	22	55.9	43	109.2
3½	89	8.9	23	58.4	44	111.8
4	102	10.2	24	61.0	45	114.3
4½	114	11.4	25	63.5	46	116.8
5	127	12.7	26	66.0	47	119.4
6	152	15.2	27	68.6	48	121.9
7	178	17.8	28	71.1	49	124.5
8	203	20.3	29	73.7	50	127.0

yards to metres

yards	metres	yards	metres	yards	metres	yards	metres	yards	metres
⅛	0.11	2⅛	1.94	4⅛	3.77	6⅛	5.60	8⅛	7.43
¼	0.23	2¼	2.06	4¼	3.89	6¼	5.72	8¼	7.54
⅜	0.34	2⅜	2.17	4⅜	4.00	6⅜	5.83	8⅜	7.66
½	0.46	2½	2.29	4½	4.11	6½	5.94	8½	7.77
⅝	0.57	2⅝	2.40	4⅝	4.23	6⅝	6.06	8⅝	7.89
¾	0.69	2¾	2.51	4¾	4.34	6¾	6.17	8¾	8.00
⅞	0.80	2⅞	2.63	4⅞	4.46	6⅞	6.29	8⅞	8.12
1	0.91	3	2.74	5	4.57	7	6.40	9	8.23
1⅛	1.03	3⅛	2.86	5⅛	4.69	7⅛	6.52	9⅛	8.34
1¼	1.14	3¼	2.97	5¼	4.80	7¼	6.63	9¼	8.46
1⅜	1.26	3⅜	3.09	5⅜	4.91	7⅜	6.74	9⅜	8.57
1½	1.37	3½	3.20	5½	5.03	7½	6.86	9½	8.69
1⅝	1.49	3⅝	3.31	5⅝	5.14	7⅝	6.97	9⅝	8.80
1¾	1.60	3¾	3.43	5¾	5.26	7¾	7.09	9¾	8.92
1⅞	1.71	3⅞	3.54	5⅞	5.37	7⅞	7.20	9⅞	9.03
2	1.83	4	3.66	6	5.49	8	7.32	10	9.14

Index

Created by Angelia McLean